Life-Study of Genesis

Messages 78-91

Witness Lee

Living Stream Ministry
Anaheim, CA • www.lsm.org

© 1976, 1977 Living Stream Ministry

All rights reserved. No part of this work may be reproduced or transmitted in any form or by any means—graphic, electronic, or mechanical, including photocopying, recording, or information storage and retrieval systems—without written permission from the publisher.

First Edition, June 1997.

ISBN 978-0-87083-914-6

Published by

Living Stream Ministry
2431 W. La Palma Ave., Anaheim, CA 92801 U.S.A.
P. O. Box 2121, Anaheim, CA 92814 U.S.A.

Printed in the United States of America

12 13 14 15 16 17 / 12 11 10 9 8 7

CONTENTS

MESSAGE SEVENTY-EIGHT **BEING** **PAGE 997**
 TRANSFORMED (1)

e. Being Transformed — 1) God's Reminding—Back to Bethel — 2) Jacob's Response — 3) God's Clearing

MESSAGE SEVENTY-NINE **BEING** **PAGE 1011**
 TRANSFORMED (2)

4) At Bethel — a) Jacob Having Built an Altar to God — b) God Appearing to Jacob — c) God Blessing Jacob — d) God Reminding Jacob of His New Name — e) God Promising Jacob — f) Jacob's Reaction to God's Promise

MESSAGE EIGHTY **BEING** **PAGE 1025**
 TRANSFORMED (3)

5) The Experience at Bethel — a) Jacob's Altar — b) God's Appearing — c) God's Blessing — d) Jacob's Experience of His New Name

MESSAGE EIGHTY-ONE **BEING** **PAGE 1037**
 TRANSFORMED (4)

e) God's Promise — (1) Not in Padan-aram — (2) Not in Succoth or in Shechem — (3) Only in Bethel

MESSAGE EIGHTY-TWO **BEING** **PAGE 1049**
 TRANSFORMED (5)

f) Jacob's Doing — (1) Building a Pillar — (a) A General Sketch — aa. For the Temple — bb. For the Building of the Church — cc. In the New Jerusalem — dd. The Need to Be in Bethel — ee. Coming to Bethel Twice — ff. The Christ on Whom We Rest Being Constituted into a Pillar — gg. Being Perfected to Be a Pillar

MESSAGE EIGHTY-THREE   BEING   PAGE 1063
                          TRANSFORMED (6)

(b) Related to the Building of the Temple — aa. By Solomon through Hiram — bb. Two Pillars — cc. Of Brass — dd. Eighteen Cubits High Apiece — ee. Twelve Cubits Round — ff. Two Capitals — gg. Nets of Checkerwork and Wreaths of Chainwork — hh. The Capitals Being of Lily Work — ii. Two Hundred Pomegranates — jj. The Capitals Being Four Cubits in Diameter — kk. Two Pillars Standing in the Porch of the Temple

MESSAGE EIGHTY-FOUR   BEING   PAGE 1079
                         TRANSFORMED (7)

ll. Two Bowls of the Two Capitals on the Top of the Two Pillars, Two Cubits High — mm. Four Hundred Pomegranates on the Two Networks — nn. Out of One Hundred Pomegranates, Ninety-six Being Exposed to the Open Air — oo. Of the Four Hundred Pomegranates, Sixteen (Four of Each Hundred) Being Hidden — pp. The Pillars Being Hollow and Their Thickness Being Four Fingers — qq. The Two Pillars Measured with One Height of Thirty-five Cubits with One Cubit Covered — rr. The Network and the Chainwork on the Two Capitals Being Seven on Each — ss. The Number Three Being Hidden — tt. The Brass, the Lily, and the Pomegranates All Being on the Two Pillars

MESSAGE EIGHTY-FIVE   THE BUILDER OF   PAGE 1091
                         THE PILLARS—
                         THE SKILLFUL
                         HIRAM (1)

I. HIS MOTHER BEING A WOMAN OF THE DAUGHTERS OF DAN   (1092)

II. HIS FATHER BEING A TYRIAN   (1095)

III. THE MARRIAGE OF HIS PARENTS BEING AGAINST GOD'S HOLY REGULATION   (1095)

IV. BECOMING ONE OF THE TRIBE OF NAPHTALI   (1096)

   A. A Hind Set Free — *1. Trusting and Rejoicing in God* — *2. Walking upon High Places* — *3. Living in Resurrection* — B. Giving Beautiful Words

V. HIS TYRIAN FATHER DYING AND HIS DANITE MOTHER BECOMING WIDOWED   (1098)

MESSAGE EIGHTY-SIX	THE BUILDER OF THE PILLARS— THE SKILLFUL HIRAM (2)	PAGE 1105

VI. HIRAM'S TRANSFER TO THE TRIBE OF NAPHTALI BEING MYSTERIOUS (1106)

VII. THE TYRIAN FATHER, THE SOURCE OF SECULAR SKILL, HAVING TO DIE THAT THE SON WHO LEARNED THIS SKILL THROUGH THE WORLDLY FATHER MAY BE RELEASED FROM THE WORLDLY TIE (1109)

VIII. THE DANITE MOTHER, SIGNIFYING HUMAN EXISTENCE, REMAINING AS A WIDOW (1112)

IX. THE SECULAR SKILL BEING USEFUL FOR GOD'S BUILDING ONLY IN RESURRECTION AFTER THE WORLDLY FATHER HAS DIED AND THE LEARNED SON HAS BEEN TRANSFERRED TO THE TRIBE OF NAPHTALI (1116)

X. THE TRANSFERRED NAPHTALITE NEEDING TO BE FETCHED OUT OF TYRE AND TO COME TO KING SOLOMON IN JERUSALEM WHERE GOD'S BUILDING IS (1116)

XI. THE CASES OF MOSES WITH JOSHUA AND PAUL WITH TIMOTHY (1117)

MESSAGE EIGHTY-SEVEN	BEING TRANSFORMED (8)	PAGE 1119

(c) Related to the Building of the Church — (d) Consummated in the New Jerusalem

MESSAGE EIGHTY-EIGHT	THE WAY TO BE PERFECTED AS A PILLAR	PAGE 1133

OUR NEED TO BE IN TODAY'S BETHEL (1133)

A PERSONAL TESTIMONY (1133)

ONE FLOW (1135)

THE MINISTRY RESPONSIBLE FOR THE FLOW (1135)

THE SECRET TO BEING PERFECTED TO BE A PILLAR (1136)

FEASTING ON THE POSITIVE THINGS (1137)

FINDING THE FLOW AND GETTING INTO IT (1139)

MESSAGE EIGHTY-NINE   **BEING**   **PAGE 1141**
TRANSFORMED (9)

(2) Pouring a Drink Offering upon the Pillar — (3) Pouring Oil upon the Pillar — (4) Realizing Bethel

MESSAGE NINETY   **BEING**   **PAGE 1153**
TRANSFORMED (10)

6) Deeper and More Personal Dealings — 7) Entering into Fellowship — 8) Released from the Tie with His Father

MESSAGE NINETY-ONE   **THE THREE**   **PAGE 1165**
PILLARS AND
THE ONE TOWER
IN JACOB'S LIFE

I. THE THREE PILLARS   (1165)

A. The Pillar at Gilead — B. The Pillar at Bethel — C. The Pillar on the Way to Bethlehem

II. THE ONE TOWER   (1175)

LIFE-STUDY OF GENESIS

MESSAGE SEVENTY-EIGHT

BEING TRANSFORMED

(1)

The Bible begins with God's creation and ends with God's habitation. We all need to be impressed with these two words—creation and habitation. The consummation of the Bible is God's eternal dwelling place. If we would know the Bible, we must keep these two things, God's creation and His habitation, firmly in mind. We have seen that the book of Genesis contains nearly all the seeds of the truths concerning God's economy. Perhaps the last seed in this book is the seed of Bethel, God's habitation. Not only at the conclusion of the Bible, but even in the latter part of Genesis, we have the consummate end of God's economy—Bethel, God's dwelling place. The word Bethel means the house of God, or the temple of God, the dwelling place of God.

The book of Genesis covers the biographies of eight great persons: Adam, Abel, Enosh, Enoch, Noah, Abraham, Isaac, and Jacob with Joseph. We must include Joseph's life as part of Jacob's. In Adam, we have God's creation, and in Jacob, we have God's habitation, Bethel. With Jacob we do not merely see God's selection. Most Christian teachers have spent considerable time on the matter of God's selection of Jacob. Yes, God's selection is the beginning, but what is the ending, the consummate goal, of God's selection? It is Bethel, God's dwelling place. God created, selected, called, and saved us for the purpose that He might have a dwelling place for eternity. This seed of the building, like all the other seeds in the book of Genesis, is developed throughout the whole Bible. If we would understand the significance of this seed, we must consider the entire Bible.

Following Jacob, we have the house of Israel. The house of Israel was actually the house of God. After the exodus from Egypt, there was among the house of Israel the building of the tabernacle, and following the tabernacle, there was the building of the temple. Hence, the Old Testament is a record of eight great men, from Adam through Jacob, plus the tabernacle and the temple. The construction, destruction, and rebuilding of the temple bring us to the end of the Old Testament. What do we have in the New Testament? Again, we have two main things: the tabernacle, which was Jesus (John 1:14), and the temple, which is the church (1 Cor. 3:16). The consummation of the church as the temple is the New Jerusalem. One meaningful and simple way of memorizing the Bible is to remember the eight great men from Adam through Jacob, the tabernacle and the temple as the types in the Old Testament, and the tabernacle and the temple as the reality in the New Testament, the ultimate issue of which is the New Jerusalem. These thirteen items cover the entire Bible.

What is the subject of the Bible? Some may say that it is man's fall, God's redemption, our repentance, God's forgiveness, our regeneration, and our salvation. Obviously, all these things are found in the Bible. Others may point out that the Bible mentions things such as serpents, scorpions, and frogs. The Bible, containing more than a thousand chapters, is not a simple book. Even one chapter may contain many points. But what is the subject of the Bible? Studying the Bible is similar to studying a human being. Although medical students have studied anatomy and physiology for centuries, they have not exhausted the study of the human body, one-third of a human being. They know something about man's body, but nothing about the soul and the human spirit. Man is very complicated. Nevertheless, he is still a man, a complete unit. We cannot refer to a man as being a heart, a kidney, or a nose. A man has a nose, but he is not the nose and the nose is not the man. Some say that the subject of the Bible is justification. Justification is included in the Bible, but it is no more the subject of the Bible than a man's nose is the man himself. If we would know what the subject of the Bible is, we must see that the Bible tells us of eight men, beginning with Adam in God's creation through Jacob with God's house, Bethel, and that following this we have the tabernacle and the temple in the Old Testament and the reality of the tabernacle and the temple in the New Testament, consummating in the New Jerusalem. Revelation 21 says that the New Jerusalem is the tabernacle of God and that God and the Lamb are the temple in it. Hence, the New Jerusalem is the ultimate issue of Bethel.

e. Being Transformed

At the time of chapter thirty-five, Jacob must have been approximately a hundred years of age. Although Jacob had passed through many things, prior to this chapter, we are not told that he had ever made a thorough clearance. He suffered many things in relation to his brother, his uncle, and his cousins, suffering twenty years under the hand of his uncle Laban. But Genesis never says that as Jacob was undergoing those sufferings he purified himself or made a clearance of himself. Rather, we are told of Jacob's skill and supplanting. But, as we shall see, when God told him to arise and go up to Bethel, Jacob made a thorough clearance.

The first time God appeared to Jacob was in a dream (28:10-22) in which Jacob saw heaven opened and a ladder extending from earth to heaven with angels ascending and descending upon it. When Jacob awoke from his sleep, he was inspired to call the name of that place Bethel, and the stone that he had used as his pillow he set up for a pillar and poured oil upon it. Following this, he vowed that if God would bring him back safely to the land of his fathers, then the stone which he had set up for a pillar would be God's house (28:22). In this dream God paid Jacob a gracious visitation and caused him, undoubtedly in the spirit, to speak concerning God's eternal economy. If Jacob had not been inspired by the Spirit of God, how could he, a supplanter, have spoken a word revealing God's eternal purpose? It would have been impossible. God unveiled to Jacob His heart's desire, which is to have Bethel.

However, that dream at Bethel did not change Jacob at all. It seems that after the dream had transpired, the inspiration returned to heaven. Jacob's manner of life was unaffected.

It is the same with us. At Bethel, Jacob prophesied in a wonderful way, speaking of God's house, but it seems that the prophecy returned to heaven. Like Jacob, many of us have had a dream, a revelation, or an inspiration in which we uttered a word of prophecy, if not to men, then at least to angels. But the next day we continued to live the same as always. After his dream at Bethel, Jacob continued his supplanting, especially the supplanting of Laban, as if he had never had the dream. In fact, he was even more "Jacobean" after the dream than before.

In chapter thirty-three, Jacob was still Jacob. The heavenly dream and the sufferings had not changed him. But something occurred in chapter thirty-four that touched Jacob's heart. His only daughter became defiled, and his sons caused him trouble by slaughtering people and plundering their city. These events touched Jacob deeply and caused him to make a radical turn. After this, God came in to speak to him.

1) God's Reminding—Back to Bethel

God did not give Jacob a sermon. Rather, because Jacob's heart had been touched and, as a result, he was ready to hear the word of God, God simply said, "Arise, go up to Bethel, and dwell there; and make there an altar unto God, that appeared unto thee when thou fleddest from the face of Esau thy brother" (35:1). Here we see that God told Jacob to do four things: to arise, to go up to Bethel, to dwell there, and to make there an altar to God who had appeared to him. The turn, or the change, Jacob made in chapter thirty-five was very significant.

2) Jacob's Response

In 35:2-7 we see Jacob's response to God's word. Before this chapter, there is no record of a man who was walking in the presence of God and who cleared himself and his whole household. Verse 2 says, "Then Jacob said unto his household, and to all that were with him, Put away the foreign gods that are among you, and purify yourselves, and change your garments" (Heb.). For the single purpose of going up to Bethel, Jacob and everyone with him had to make a thorough clearance and to purify themselves. In this chapter God did not say, "Jacob, you are going to Bethel to build an altar there; you should realize that you must be holy. I am holy, and you must be holy also. You must rid yourself of all your foreign gods, purify yourself of every defilement, and change your garments."

Recently, an elderly Christian, a man who had been a preacher for over forty years, asked if we teach our people to dress in a certain way. He had observed the way the brothers and sisters dressed and wondered if we taught them to do so. I told him that during the past fourteen years we had never laid down any regulations about clothing. However, anyone who has been touched by God for His dwelling place will sense that something within is charging him to clear himself and to purify himself. You may tolerate certain defilements and looseness in your life. But whenever you touch the church and you mean business with the Lord to have the church life, something within charges you concerning those things which are not fitting for the church life. Immediately after God commanded Jacob to arise and go up to Bethel, Jacob charged his people to get rid of the foreign gods, to purify themselves, and to change their garments. Later we shall see that changing the garments signifies changing our manner of life, that is, putting off the old manner of life and putting on a new man. Although God did not tell Jacob to do this, something deep within him required this of him. If he had been charged to go to a worldly place, he would have sensed no need to purify himself. Rather, he would have been ready to defile himself even more. Jacob had such a radical change because he had been touched for Bethel, for God's eternal dwelling place.

a) Making a Thorough Clearance

(1) Putting Away Their Foreign Gods—Idols

Firstly, Jacob told his household and all that were with him to put away the foreign gods that were among them (35:2). When Jacob and his household were fleeing from Laban, Rachel took the household images (31:34-35). Prior to chapter thirty-five, Jacob never charged Rachel to put them away. But after God had told him to go up to Bethel, everyone had to abandon their foreign gods, their idols. This is a shadow, a type, that is developed throughout the Bible. According to both the Old Testament and the New Testament, the first thing we must eliminate for the sake of God's dwelling place is our idols.

Many may claim that they have never had anything to do with idols. Materially speaking, it may be true to say that you have no idols. But we must know, spiritually speaking, what an idol is. An idol is anything that replaces God. Your education, your ambition, your position, your name, your desire, and your intention may replace God in your life and thus become idols. If you view the matter in this light, then you will have to admit that you have had many foreign gods. If your relative or friend replaces God in your life, then he is an idol to you. Our parents, spouses, and children may all become our idols.

Do you know why people worship idols? Undoubtedly, they worship them because of Satan's seduction. But there is a reason on the human side why people do this. People worship idols for the sake of gaining long life and happiness. Satan threatens people, telling them that if they do not worship idols, they will not have long life and happiness, but that if they worship idols, then they will have long life and happiness. Happiness includes many things: money, position, ambition, fame, a name. Many have idols due to their desire to be healthy. Why do you have something that replaces God? Simply because that thing may make you happy. Unlike Rachel, Jacob had no literal idols, but in his supplanting he had some idols. In fact, his supplanting was an idol. Why did Jacob supplant others? Because of his desire for happiness and enjoyment. Today, man has lost God and, pursuing foreign gods, seeks his happiness in idols. But God is our long life and happiness.

When God spoke to Jacob regarding Bethel, Jacob received the revelation concerning his life and realized that his life on earth was not for his own happiness. His life was for Bethel, for God's house. Thus, Bethel became his goal, the destination of his human life on earth. Formerly, his goal was his own happiness. Now, his goal and destination were replaced. No longer was his goal something for himself but something absolutely for God. In Shechem, Jacob had everything. But due to the trouble caused by his sons, he lost his safety and peace. At that juncture, God seemed to say, "Jacob, go up to My house. Here in Shechem you don't have safety and peace. Safety and peace are at Bethel. You must go up there." Thus, Bethel became Jacob's goal and destination. Jacob realized that the goal of God's house was holy; it was not a common thing. No one could enter into the house of God with idols, pollution, and old, filthy garments. Therefore, Jacob charged his household and everyone with him to put away all the foreign gods.

(2) Purifying Themselves

Jacob also charged everyone to purify themselves (35:2). We must not only put away the foreign gods but also purify our whole being. In other words, our whole being, manner of life, and expression must be changed. This is not merely regeneration or a little change in life. Rather, it is a full transformation. Here in Genesis 35, Jacob was transformed.

In the Bible, purifying ourselves means to be purified from every pollution. Our whole being must be cleansed from anything that is pollution in the eyes of God. In 2 Corinthians 7:1 Paul says, "Therefore, having these promises, beloved, let us cleanse ourselves from all defilement of flesh and spirit, perfecting holiness in the fear of God." Paul's concept in 2 Corinthians 6 and 7 was the same as Jacob's in Genesis 35. Because the Corinthians were the temple of God, Paul told them to purify themselves. There can be no agreement between the temple of God and idols (2 Cor. 6:16). Idols are idols, and the temple of God is the temple of God. Which side do you take? If idols, then go to your idols. If the temple of God, then come to the temple without any idols.

When you came into the church life, no one told you anything, but deep within something convinced you that certain things had to go for the sake of the proper church life. Every one of us had such a clearance upon coming into the church. At that time, we cleared away many, if not all, of the foreign gods, forsaking the things, the matters, and even the persons we trusted in for happiness, saying, "I don't like to keep these things anymore. All foreign idols must go." In the church life, not an inch of ground can be surrendered to foreign gods. Furthermore, when we came into the church life we were purified. At least, we aspired to be pure, saying, "For the sake of the church life, I want to be pure in my whole being, in my mind, emotion, and will." We had the same desire that Jacob had. On the day Jacob's people went up to Bethel, they purified themselves, and among them there were no foreign gods.

Many of us, including myself, realize that we are not very good. Perhaps even today you have said, "Oh, I am not so good. My thinking is still not very pure." However, compare your present manner of life with your past. Although you should not be proud of yourself, you should say, "Lord, thank You. I am not very pleased with myself, but as I compare the present with the past, I have to thank and praise You that I am quite different from what I was." Although in chapter thirty-five Jacob was not yet mature, he had undoubtedly changed from what he once was. In the next message we shall see how radically transformed Jacob actually was. God again changed his name from Jacob to Israel. God told him that he should no longer call himself Jacob but Israel.

I have known many of you for twelve years or more. I know that many of you are unhappy with yourselves today. When someone asks you how you are doing, according to custom, you say, "I'm fine." According to your inner sense, however, you are not so fine. Perhaps you have just repented, crying to the Lord; but when someone asks you how you are, you say that you are fine. Although you may say "fine" to a brother, you never say this to the Lord. We should neither be proud nor disappointed. Compare yourself with what you were twelve years ago. Has there not been a great change? Who changed us? We all must admit that we did not change ourselves; we were changed by being in Bethel, in the church life. If you deliberately stay away from the church life for a few weeks, your former ugliness will return, the fox tail will become visible, the serpent tongue will be exercised, and all the bugs will be active. But if you continue coming to the church, contacting the church again and again, the fox tail will be removed, the serpent tongue will be cut off, and the bugs will be poisoned. As long as you come to the church, the bugs will all be exterminated.

The church life is the most effective purification. Recently, I experienced a great deal of purification in the prayer meeting. As I was sitting in the meeting joining in the prayers, I was bathed and purified. I would not say that I was purified by the prayers, but I was purified by the church. The church is a large bathroom where we all are bathed and purified. If the church does not have this function, I am fearful that it will not long remain the church. As long as the church is the church, it will function this way. Often, when it is time to go to the church meeting, something within begins to purify us, telling us to cleanse ourselves. On our way to the meeting, we have frequently prayed, "Lord, I'm going to the meeting. Forgive me of this, cleanse me of that matter, and take that away from me." This is the purification for going up to Bethel. Let us all purify ourselves, for we must arise, go up to Bethel, and meet our God. We cannot meet Him in an old, polluted way. We must be purified. This purification is not a matter of our working, but of the working of the divine hand upon us. When we take care of His Bethel, His divine hand will purify us.

(3) Changing Their Garments

In addition to putting away the foreign gods and purifying themselves, they changed their garments (35:2). According to the Bible, to change garments means to change your manner of life. Ephesians 4:22-24 reveals that the old manner of life was the life of the fallen humanity and that the new manner of life is of the church. The church is the regenerated, new creation, and humanity is the fallen, old creation. When we were unsaved, we lived a manner of life that was of the fallen, old creation. Now, after having been saved and regenerated and having been brought into the church life, we must have a new manner of life. We must put off the old man and put on the new man. To put off the old man is to put off the old garments, the old manner of life, and to put on the new man is to put on the new manner of life, the church.

After putting away the foreign gods and purifying ourselves, we must change our garments, changing our manner of life. We should no longer express ourselves in an old way, but express ourselves as the church, as the new man in the new manner of life. We were the old, fallen creation, but now we are the new, regenerated creation. Many of our relatives, friends, colleagues, and neighbors can testify that after we came into the church life, our manner of life drastically changed. The church has changed and continues to change our manner of life. This is for Bethel.

(4) Burying Their Earrings

Verse 4 says, "And they gave unto Jacob all the foreign gods which were in their hand, and all their earrings which were in their ears; and Jacob hid them under the oak which was by Shechem" (Heb.). Not only were the idols buried, but also the earrings. Earrings are self-beautifying items. These were dealt with in the same way as the idols. Many people's earrings, ornaments, are equal to idols in the eyes of God. When those in Jacob's household were putting away the foreign gods, they also put away their earrings. This indicates that to their conscience their earrings were as abominable as their foreign gods. After touching the church, many sisters had the same conviction and put off this kind of abominable ornament. This is not something related to morality but to the house of God.

God did not charge Jacob to make such a clearance. Still less did He say, "Jacob, you must tell your household and everyone with you to make a clearance and to purify themselves." Why, then, did Jacob charge everyone in this way? Because the house of God is not an individual matter. It is not only Jacob. The house of God must be the house of Jacob becoming the house of Israel. Eventually, all the descendants of Jacob became the house of God, Bethel. The real Bethel was not the tabernacle; it was the children of Israel. Likewise, we must see that today we are the church. We must be purified not only because we are going to Bethel, but because we are to be Bethel. We must put away all foreign gods and abominable ornaments, purify ourselves, and change our garments. Putting away the foreign gods also means putting away all foreign trusts. We must be cleansed in our whole being, inwardly and outwardly, from every pollution, and we must change our manner of life. This is all for the church life.

(5) Terrifying the Enemies

Verse 5 says, "And they journeyed: and the terror of God was upon the cities that were round about them, and they did not pursue after the sons of Jacob." It is very encouraging to see that their enemies were terrified. Due to the trouble caused by his sons, Jacob was afraid that the city people would fight against him and kill him. But after Jacob and all those with him had put away the idols, purified themselves, and changed their garments, a terror from God fell upon the city people. Their clearance and purification terrified the enemy. This indicates that if, for the sake of the church life, we put away all foreign gods and self-beautifying and abominable ornaments, purify ourselves, and change our garments, the demons and besetting sins will be terrified. There will be no need to fight to overcome; the enemy will be terrified and the victory will be ours. Have you ever terrified sins? Have you ever terrified gambling, drinking, or smoking? Perhaps you have found these things difficult to overcome. If so, it is because you have not put away foreign gods, purified yourselves, and changed your garments. If you do all this, all the "bugs," "scorpions," and "gophers" will be terrified and will flee and hide. I have read some books about overcoming sin and the world. Forty or fifty years ago I practiced what I read in those books. But the more I practiced, the more defeated I was because I was not in the church. Being in the church by putting away the foreign trusts, purifying ourselves, and changing our garments terrifies sin and worldliness and gives us the victory. Are you troubled by the little "gopher" of your temper? It will be terrified. Genesis 35:5 says that the people of the cities did not dare to pursue Jacob. God gave Jacob a prosperous journey up to Bethel. Whenever we are in the church, all the "gophers" are terrified.

b) Going Up to Bethel

After making a thorough clearance, Jacob and all his people arose and went up to Bethel (vv. 3, 6). At Bethel, he built an altar to God and "called the place El-Beth-el" (v. 7), realizing that God was God to him at Bethel. We must respond to God's call or reminder to go up to the church where we can build the altar of our real consecration and experience God in a practical way. After we come into the church, we all realize the need of a real consecration. By such a consecration, we experience God being God to us in His house—the church.

3) God's Clearing

Verse 8 says, "Deborah, Rebekah's nurse died, and she was buried beneath Bethel under an oak: and the name of it was called Allon-bachuth." For quite a while, I could not understand why, at this juncture, Deborah, Rebekah's nurse, died. There are no wasted words in the Bible. Deborah was a nurse to Jacob's mother, Rebekah. Rebekah must have died prior to Jacob's return. Thus, Deborah must have been very dear to Jacob as a comfort in place of his mother. At the precise time Jacob had the experience of Bethel, Deborah, his comfort, was taken away by God. As many of us can testify, when we put away the foreign gods, purified ourselves, changed our garments, and came into the church life, God intervened to take away our "Deborahs," our nursing mothers. Many of us had a "Deborah," someone or something loving, sympathizing, and soothing. But the day we came into the church life God spontaneously took our nurse away, and our "Deborah" died. The church life is a life that does not require a nurse. None of the church people needs a nursing mother. But, sorry to say, some of us still like to have some nurses to sympathize with us and to soothe and to comfort us like a mother taking care of an infant. Any word spoken positively regarding nursing mothers is addressed to babes. After being in the church for so long, do you still need someone to nurse you? Nevertheless, even the older ones still desire a "Deborah" to soothe and care for them. But if we mean business with the Lord for Bethel, He will remove our nurses.

In these verses we see that three things were buried: the idols, the earrings, and the nurse. All were buried under an oak. The oak is a symbol of flourishing life. Hence, all the foreign gods, the self-beautifying items, and the nurses are buried under the flourishing life, especially the life in the church. This is not a doctrine, but something that corresponds to our experience. The life in the church flourishes like an oak tree, but underneath it are the "Deborahs." We put off the idols and removed the earrings, but God caused our "Deborah" to die. This is a real purification, both from our side and from God's side. We put away and God took away. We put away the foreign gods, the earrings, the pollutions, and garments, and God took away the nurses. In the church life we do not need sympathy or nursing. All our "Deborahs" must be buried.

The oak under which Deborah was buried was "beneath Bethel" (v. 8). This indicates that our experience of the taking away and the burying of our "Deborahs" is not on a high plane; rather, it is beneath the level of the church. The church as the house of God is on the highest plane, and here in the church we must have some experiences that are also on the highest plane, such as the experience of Christ as our life and our person. To experience the burial of our "Deborahs" is rather low; it is beneath Bethel. Hence, the burial oak was called Allon-bachuth—the oak of weeping. This is not a matter worthy of our rejoicing.

LIFE-STUDY OF GENESIS

MESSAGE SEVENTY-NINE

BEING TRANSFORMED

(2)

Genesis contains the seeds of nearly all the truths in the Bible. If we observe this principle, whenever we come to certain points in this book, we shall recognize that they are developed in the following books of the Bible. In other words, in order to understand any point in Genesis, we need to trace its development elsewhere in the Scriptures. Without the other books, we simply cannot understand Genesis. Genesis is not merely a book of stories. If we would derive the life, the supply, the revelation, and the vision from all the points found in the book of Genesis, then we must follow their development in all the subsequent books of the Bible.

The truth concerning the house of God was sown in chapter twenty-eight. If you read the Bible carefully, you will see that the house of God was first mentioned in this chapter. The house of God, Bethel, is mentioned in relation to a vision granted to Jacob in a very extraordinary way. Firstly, Jacob had a dream and then his dream was interpreted under divine inspiration. In his dream, Jacob saw the heavens open and a ladder set up on the earth extending from earth to heaven. Upon the ladder the angels of God were ascending and descending. With any dream, we firstly have the facts in the dream and then the proper interpretation. Jacob did not have a Daniel to interpret his dream for him; instead, this supplanter became his own Daniel. He certainly did an excellent job interpreting his dream, saying, "How dreadful is this place! this is none other but the house of God, and this is the gate of heaven" (28:17). Jacob said that this place, Bethel, was dreadful. If you would go to heaven, you must pass through this dreadful place, for the house of God is the gate of heaven.

After his dream, Jacob also made a vow, saying, "If God will be with me, and will keep me in this way that I go, and will give me bread to eat, and raiment to put on, so that I come again to my father's house in peace; then shall the Lord be my God" (28:20-21). Instead of speaking to God in an intimate prayer, he made a vow. As part of his vow, Jacob said that the stone which he had set up for a pillar would be God's house (28:22). In Jacob's vow we see a further interpretation of his dream. Upon waking, Jacob said that that place was the house of God. Then he promised that the stone he used for a pillow would be built up into God's house. We see here that the house of God will be built with the stone which was Jacob's trust. The stone that Jacob used as a pillow is a shadow, a prefigure, a type, of Christ. Only Christ is the real rock that can be the pillow upon which we can lay our weary head. The very Christ on whom we rest will become the house of God. This is the material for building the house of God. In Genesis 28 we have the first mention of the stone for God's building. Of course, in chapter two the onyx stone is mentioned, but it is not mentioned in a clear way. The stone which is our trust will become the house of God. This means that the Christ whom we experience as our rest and trust will become the building material for God's house.

In chapter thirty-five the vision of Bethel came again. This time, however, it did not come just as a dream; it came as a reality. It was not only a vision, but a fact and an experience. The difference between chapters twenty-eight and thirty-five is that chapter twenty-eight was merely a dream. Bethel, the gate of heaven, the ladder, the angels—everything was seen in a dream. At most, we can only say that this dream was a vision. Up to that point there was no fact, no reality. The fulfillment of the dream comes into being in chapter thirty-five.

4) At Bethel

In this message we need to consider Jacob's experience at Bethel (35:6-7, 9-15). In Genesis 35 Jacob underwent a major change. As we saw in the last message, Jacob reacted to God's charge to arise and go up to Bethel by having a thorough clearance. This thorough clearance was not only made by him but by all those who were with him. Jacob was not only concerned with himself but with everyone with him. This is a strong proof that he had had a radical and thorough change. Undoubtedly, Jacob had been transformed.

a) Jacob Having Built an Altar to God

Jacob came to Bethel, "he and all the people that were with him. And he built there an altar, and called the place El-Beth-el" (vv. 6-7). The first thing Jacob did at Bethel was to build an altar. Although Jacob had built an altar in Shechem, he did not call that altar "El-Shechem." He could not use the title of God for the altar he built in Shechem. This means that the altar in Shechem did not touch God's heart; it was not the altar He desired. Likewise, we may build altars everywhere without building the altar God desires. You may build an altar in Las Vegas, but you cannot call it the altar of God in Las Vegas. But when Jacob acted on the word of God, arising, going up to Bethel, dwelling there, and building an altar to God, he built an altar according to God's desires, not according to his own intention. God did not ask him to build an altar in Shechem, for that was not His choice. God's desire was to bring him back to Bethel. Thus, the altar built by Jacob in Shechem was neither according to God's desire nor according to His word. But because the altar Jacob built in Bethel was built at the word of God, he had the boldness to call it "El-Beth-el."

You may do many things for God, such as preaching the gospel and rendering other service to Him. You may even establish a meeting and designate it as the church. However, you do not have the confidence or the boldness to say that that is something of God. This is even true in small things. For example, you may love a brother, but not have the boldness to call that love the love of God. Although you do love that brother, you do not love him at God's word. Rather, you love him by your own choice and according to your personal taste. Because it is your love, you cannot say that it is "El-love," the love of God. You cannot call it the love of God until you love people at God's word and not according to your taste. When God tells you to love a certain brother, you must love him at His word. If you love the brother in this way, then your love will be the love of God.

Many missionaries have gone to the mission field without having the assurance that their mission was "El-mission." Many have told me that while they were working they had no peace. They did not have the confidence, assurance, or boldness to say that their mission work was the work of God. They were doubtful about it and could not attach God's name to it.

Many Christians today are forming groups. The larger groups become denominations and the smaller groups remain free groups. However, the founders of those groups do not have the confidence to call them the church. But when we in the Lord's recovery say that we are the church, they are offended. Deep within them, they lack the assurance to say that they are the church. A man is a man, and a woman is a woman. You cannot call a man a woman. Fifty years ago I began to say, "This is the church." The more I said this, the more confident I became because this really is the church. If it is not the church, then what is it? I am a man. The more I say that I am a man, the more assured I am of being a man. If you do not call me a man, then what would you call me? You may do many different things—start a mission work, establish a meeting, form a Bible study—but it all may simply be a good work done in Shechem, not in Bethel. Hence, you cannot call that work "El-Beth-el." However, when Jacob built the altar in Bethel, he had the boldness to call it "El-Beth-el."

The significance of an altar is consecration. An altar is built for the purpose of offering things to God. Before I came into the church life, I thoroughly consecrated myself to the Lord. However, after coming into the church life, I renewed my consecration. This renewed consecration was absolutely different from the consecration I had made prior to coming into the church life. Many of us can testify to this. You might have offered yourselves to the Lord many times before coming into the church, but once you came into the church, you had the deep conviction that you needed to offer yourselves anew and that there was a great difference between this consecration and any previous one. At best, your past consecration was at the altar in Shechem; it was not at the altar in Bethel. Consecration made before coming into the church is one thing, and the consecration made within the church is another.

b) God Appearing to Jacob

After the altar was built, God appeared to Jacob again (v. 9). Jacob's experience was somewhat different from Abraham's. When God first appeared to Abraham, there was no altar. But God appeared to Jacob, not only at Bethel, but in front of the altar. Before we came into the church life, we did have some experience of God's appearing. However, we were not at Bethel in front of the altar. Being by the altar at Bethel makes a great difference. Now, after coming into the church and building an altar, God appears again. Many of us can testify that after coming into the church life and consecrating ourselves to the Lord anew, we had the deep conviction that the Lord had appeared to us. We had the appearing of the Lord in our personal experience. It was not a mere doctrine. As long as we have built an altar at Bethel, we should have the appearing of God. This should not happen once in a while; it must be a continual experience. Daily and even hourly, we should experience the appearing of the Lord. In other words, we should walk in the Lord's presence.

c) God Blessing Jacob

When God appeared to Jacob in Bethel, He blessed him (v. 9). What blessing we have received since coming to Bethel and building an altar! When I was young, I liked the hymn that says, "Count your blessings, name them one by one." I encourage you to count your blessings, making a list of all the blessings you have experienced in the church life. How profound are the blessings in the church! Outside the church, no one can have the blessings found in Bethel.

d) God Reminding Jacob of His New Name

In His appearing to Jacob at Bethel, God also reminded him of his new name, saying, "Thy name is Jacob: thy name shall not be called anymore Jacob, but Israel shall be thy name; and he called his name Israel" (v. 10). God seemed to be saying, "Jacob, didn't I change your name? Why then do you still call yourself Jacob? Now I remind you that your name is no longer Jacob and that you must call yourself Israel. Don't call yourself Jacob anymore, for that means that you live, walk, behave, and have your being in a 'Jacobean' way. You must live, walk, and have your being like Israel. Don't you know that you have wrestled with Me and have overcome Me? You must show the universe that you are an overcomer. You are not only a prince of God, but a wrestler of God. You must live in this way." This reminder had a background: the trouble caused by Jacob's sons and Jacob's fear and loss of boldness. Although he had been bold to wrestle with God, he was timid in facing the city people. In fact, he was terrified of them. But in reminding him of his new name, Israel, God seemed to say, "You don't need to be afraid of them. If you are afraid, it means that you have forgotten the name I gave you. I have given you the name 'the wrestler of God.' If you can wrestle with God, then you certainly can wrestle with anyone. If you can overcome Me, then whom can't you overcome? Jacob, you don't need to be afraid of anyone. I have given you the name Israel. I was not offended by your wrestling with Me; rather, I appreciated it. Thus, I have given you the name 'the wrestler of God.' From now on, you should not be a supplanter, but a wrestler of God. Wherever you go, you must proclaim, 'I am the wrestler of God! The wrestler of God comes!' Jacob, behave yourself like a wrestler of God. Why must you be so timid? After you took My word to come here to Bethel, all the city people were terrified of you. You don't need to be afraid of them. Why should you be Jacob anymore? Forget about being Jacob and call yourself Israel."

The name Jacob means supplanter, heel-holder. Which do you want to be—a supplanter or a wrestler of God? Our original name was Jacob, but now our name is Israel. Do you believe this? If you do, then why are you still afraid of your temper? Why do you not rise up and say, "Temper, you must know that I am a wrestler of God. I am Israel." Whatever you fear will become your portion. If you are afraid of losing your temper, be assured that you will lose it. But if you tell your temper that you are Israel, the wrestler of God, the little "bug" of temper will disappear. Some of you may say, "I don't feel that I am Israel." No one asked you to feel it. God did not say to Jacob, "Jacob, don't you feel that you are Israel?" If God had done this, Jacob certainly would have replied, "No, I never feel like I am Israel. According to my feeling, I am still Jacob." Take heed to God's word. Which is more trustworthy—your feeling or God's word? Forget your feelings, considerations, understanding, and natural sight and listen to God's word and to His reminder. God has already said that our name should be called Israel. Why then are you still Jacob? From now on, we all must be Israel. Here in Bethel, Jacob began to call himself Israel. Would you say that you are Israel? Do you have the boldness to proclaim this, or do you still say that you are so weak? We are at Bethel and we are Israel. Both Bethel and Israel end with the letters e-l, indicating that both names imply the name of God. Do not look at yourself; listen to His reminder. This should encourage us and prepare us for God's promise.

e) God Promising Jacob

(1) To Be Fruitful and Multiply

In verse 11 God said to Jacob, "I am God, all-sufficient: be fruitful and multiply" (Heb.). This is the first item of God's promise. At Bethel, God promised Jacob that he would be fruitful and multiply. All of us in the church life, including the least and the youngest, need to believe this promise and claim its fulfillment, saying, "Lord, I do not agree with being a solitary believer. I stand on Your promise to be fruitful and multiply." If you do this, after a certain time, there will be thirtyfold, then sixtyfold, and then a hundredfold. When I was young, I prayed this way many times, and the Lord has surely answered my prayers. We all must pray to be multiplied. The Lord will answer our prayer and honor His promise. The way of the Lord's recovery is narrow and will never become a mass movement. No mass movement can be of the Lord's recovery, because the Lord's recovery is a matter of a multiplying life. Look at the plants: they have life and multiply. We are living with a divine life, and this life is a multiplying life. We have the confidence that we shall multiply. Pray for this and stand on His promise, taking hold to His word. Some may say that this was only a promise given to Jacob and that none of the Old Testament promises are for us today. Literally speaking, this is true. But all the promises made to Israel are types. Since we are in the reality today, the promises in type are also for us. Stand on the Lord's word and say, "Lord, what You promised Jacob was a shadow, but it must be a reality to me."

(2) To Be a Nation with Kings

God also promised Jacob, saying, "A company of nations shall be of thee, and kings shall come out of thy loins." Firstly, we have "a company of nations," indicating multiplication, and then we have kings, indicating the kingdom. Following Jacob, there was the nation of his descendants. Then there was the kingdom of his descendants under David and Solomon. In New Testament times there was the kingdom under his descendant, Jesus Christ; in the next age there will be the millennial kingdom; and after that, the eternal kingdom in the new heaven and the new earth. This one matter of the kings requires all the subsequent books of the Old Testament and the New Testament for its fulfillment. Revelation 11:15 is a part of this promise made to Jacob: "The kingdom of the world has become the kingdom of our Lord and of His Christ, and He shall reign forever and ever." Even the church today as God's kingdom on earth is included in this promise. I am aware that when some hear this they will argue with me, saying that by mixing the church with Israel I am teaching wrongly. Literally speaking, this may be correct, but remember that everything in Jacob's life was a type to be fulfilled by us. Do not be satisfied to have one or two people saved through you. Rather, you should say, "Lord, I am not happy with this. I want to see the kingdom. I need the multiplication that will issue in the kingdom." This is a great matter. Do you have the faith for it? We all must say, "Lord, I would have the faith to be multiplied, not for my empire, but for Your kingdom."

(3) To Inherit the Land with His Seed

Still another aspect of God's promise to Jacob is mentioned in verse 12: "And the land which I gave Abraham and Isaac, to thee I will give it, and to thy seed after thee will I give the land." Here, Jacob is given the promise of inheriting the land with the seed. This promise is like a huge mountain. Do not think that the land mentioned here is simply the narrow strip of the land of Palestine. That narrow strip of land was a type of Christ as the good land. Christ as the good land for our possession eventually will be the stone that falls from heaven in Daniel 2. This stone will become a mountain filling the whole earth. Do you believe that the entire earth will be a great mountain and that there will be no plain, only a holy mountain? This great mountain is Christ.

f) Jacob's Reaction to God's Promise

In verses 14 and 15 we see Jacob's reaction to God's promise. Every time the Lord speaks to us, we must react. We should not be dull, dumb, or dead. Because I am living, I react to whatever people say. If a brother had no reaction whatever to anything I said to him, I would conclude that he was either dumb or dead. When I speak to my grandchildren, they are very active and aggressive because they are living. When God spoke to Jacob, he reacted immediately.

(1) Setting Up a Pillar of Stone

Verse 14 says that "Jacob set up a pillar in the place where he had talked with him, even a pillar of stone." The first thing that Jacob did in reacting to God's word was to repeat what he had done in Bethel the first time—to set up a pillar of stone. Nothing in our first dream that was truly of the Lord can ever be forgotten. When we return to the vision, we must repeat it. In 28:18 Jacob set up for a pillar the stone he had used for a pillow and he called the name of that pillar Bethel. He repeated this in chapter thirty-five. This is a crucial point. Deep within, Jacob was convicted that he was held by God to build Him a house on earth. Perhaps Jacob said to himself, "I could never forget my experience at Bethel. Now, after returning to Bethel, God talked to me much more than He did before. Many years ago, I set up a stone as a pillar for His house. Now, after listening to Him again, I must repeat this." Jacob had vowed that a house would be built for God on earth. Eventually, this was completed by Solomon who built the temple as God's house.

(2) Pouring a Drink Offering on the Pillar

Now we come to a very weighty matter—the pouring of the drink offering upon the pillar (v. 14). In chapter twenty-eight, Jacob poured oil upon the stone that he had set up for a pillar. But in chapter thirty-five there is some further development. Before he poured oil upon the pillar, he poured a drink offering upon it. Probably very few of us know the true significance of the drink offering. If you consult the commentaries for a definition of it, you will be unsuccessful. But by reading other verses, such as Numbers 15:1-5; 28:7-10; Philippians 2:17; and 2 Timothy 4:6, along with our experience, we can grasp the genuine significance of the drink offering.

According to Leviticus chapters one through seven, God charged His people to offer various offerings, without mentioning the drink offering because this offering was additional. Later, God charged Moses that His people, after entering into the good land, had to offer Him the drink offering in addition to the basic offerings in Leviticus 1 through 7. Hence, the drink offering was additional to the basic offerings. The basic offerings included the burnt offering, the meal offering, the peace offering, the sin offering, and the trespass offering. In addition to all these basic offerings, the children of Israel had to offer the drink offering (Num. 15:1-10; 28:7-10). (The drink offering mentioned in Exodus 29:40-41 was for the service of the priests, and the drink offering mentioned in Leviticus 23:13, 18, and 37 was for the firstfruit offered to God after the Israelites had entered into the good land and had labored on it, v. 10). In both Philippians 2:17 and 2 Timothy 4:6, Paul considered himself to be a drink offering. In Philippians 2:17 he said, "But if even I am poured out as a drink offering on the sacrifice and priestly service of your faith, I rejoice and rejoice with you all." Here Paul told the Philippians that he was being poured out as a drink offering upon their sacrifice or offering (the Greek word can be rendered either way). Paul seemed to be saying, "You Philippians are offering something to God. I am happy to be poured out as a drink offering upon your offering." Shortly before Paul was martyred he said to Timothy, "For I am already being poured out, and the time of my departure is at hand." What was the drink offering poured upon? According to the Old Testament, the drink offering was always poured out upon one of the basic offerings. When Paul was about to be martyred, upon what was he being poured out as a drink offering?

As we shall see, he was being poured out upon Christ. According to Leviticus, we may offer Christ to God as the basic offerings. By offering Christ in this way, we have some experience of Christ. This experience makes us happy, and we become people filled with joy, with new wine. As those who offer Christ to God, we shall be filled with new wine. We shall have wine within us. Eventually, this wine will saturate our entire being and we ourselves will actually become wine. When Paul said that he was being poured out as a drink offering, he himself, through his rich experience of Christ, was the wine that was being poured out as a drink offering upon the Christ he had experienced and offered to God. If you could check with the martyrs like Peter and Paul, they would all testify that their martyrdom was just a pouring out upon Christ of their joy with their whole being. All the martyrs were poured out as a drink offering upon Christ to God. They experienced Christ to such an extent that when they offered Christ to God as the basic offerings, they themselves were also poured out as a drink offering upon Christ. If we have the genuine experience of Christ day after day, this experience will fill us with joy as with divine wine. Then we shall be drunken with wine and become wine for God, saying, "O God, I would like to be poured out upon Christ as a drink offering to You." Often in the Lord's table meeting I have realized that a number of saints have experienced Christ to such a degree that when they offered Christ to God at the Lord's table, there was the indication in their prayer and praise that they were ready to pour themselves out upon Christ to God. This is the drink offering, and it can only be experienced in Bethel.

The seed of the drink offering is sown in Genesis 35. If we would understand it, we must read Numbers 15 and 28, Philippians 2:17, and 2 Timothy 4:6. Then we shall understand that we must not only offer Christ to God as the basic offerings, but also as the drink offering. We need to be filled with joy by experiencing Christ that we may become wine for God and be willing to be poured out as a drink offering upon Christ to God. This experience is deep and quite subjective. You may say, "O Father God, I offer myself as a drink offering upon Christ to You." Although you may say this, if you have not experienced Christ to the extent that you are filled with joy and are drunken with heavenly wine, you will not have the joy and the willingness to be poured out as a drink offering to God. In the church life there are the possibility and the potential of experiencing Christ so much that we shall be saturated with the divine wine and even become wine. Oh, in the church life I am filled with joy and am willing to be poured out upon Christ as a drink offering for God's satisfaction.

God enjoys drinking wine. He does not want the wine made from grapes, but the wine made from Christ's saturating us. God is not interested in grapes—He is interested in you with Christ. We must become wine through the experience of Christ. The only place where we can become God's wine is in the church. I assure you that in the church your experience of Christ will bring you to the point where you will be filled with heavenly joy and will become the divine wine and be willing to be poured out upon Christ for God's satisfaction. This is the reaction of Israel in Bethel. I have the complete confidence that from now on there will be many reactions like this in the local churches. Many dear saints will say, "Lord, I'm so saturated with Your joy that I'm drunken. I have become wine to satisfy my God. Now I am willing to be poured out, even to be martyred." Recall that Paul said that he was already being poured out upon Christ for God's satisfaction. In the church life we all must be saturated with heavenly joy so that we might be ready and willing to sacrifice ourselves, to be poured out upon Christ for God's satisfaction. In the church life we all can experience Christ to the degree that we are willing to be poured out as a drink offering.

(3) Pouring Oil upon the Pillar

As we have pointed out in chapter twenty-eight, pouring oil upon the pillar signifies the outpouring of the Spirit of God upon God's chosen people for the building of God's house. But here the pouring of the oil upon the pillar follows the pouring out of the drink offering upon the pillar. This indicates that our pouring ourselves out as a drink offering to God brings in the outpouring of the Spirit of God for His building. The more we pour out ourselves with Christ as an offering to God for His house, the more the outpouring of the Spirit of God will be brought in. The building of God's house needs this.

(4) Calling the Place Bethel

Verse 15 says, "And Jacob called the name of the place where God spake with him, Beth-el." In Genesis 28 Jacob called the place Bethel, but in Genesis 35, being convinced that it was Bethel, he again called that place by this name. The longer we remain in the church and the more we experience Christ in the church, the more we shall be assured that this is Bethel, and the more bold we shall be to say, "This is the church and I am in it." This is not simply a term, much less a designation or a denomination; it is our conviction and our declaration of the fact. We are fully assured that this is Bethel. Praise the Lord that we all can say, "I am now in Bethel. This is the church."

LIFE-STUDY OF GENESIS

MESSAGE EIGHTY

BEING TRANSFORMED

(3)

5) *The Experience at Bethel*

We have seen that many crucial seeds of the truth are sown in the book of Genesis. The house of God, Bethel, is one of these seeds. However, not many Christians know what the experience of the house of God is. Undoubtedly, many know that, according to the New Testament, the house of God denotes the church (1 Tim. 3:15). But where is the practical and proper church life? Although there are millions of Christians on earth, very few of them have the genuine church life. Many merely sit in the congregation for the Sunday morning service and listen to a minister or pastor. But this is not the practical and proper church life revealed in the Bible. According to the Bible, in the genuine church life every saved one must be a living, functioning member. Every member of the Body of Christ must function. Not only do the members function, but they also live together to express God in Christ in a living, daily way. This is the practical church life revealed in the Bible. The truths regarding this practical church life are sown as seeds in Genesis.

Prior to chapter thirty-five, God was called the God of a certain person, for example, the God of Abraham or the God of Isaac. He was the God of individual persons. But in 35:7 we have "El-Beth-el," the God of the house of God. He is no longer simply the God of individuals; He is now the God of a corporate body, the house of God. Many Christians only experience God as their individual God. Not many have the experience of God as the God of the house of God. How much experience do you have of God as the God of a corporate body?

We all must experience God in such a way that He is not only God to us individually, but also the God of the house of God. There is a great difference between the two.

In Genesis 35 we see a crucial and radical turn. However, not many children of God appreciate this. They read this chapter again and again without recognizing the radical turn contained in it. Before this chapter, God was the God of individuals. He was the God of Abel, the God of Enosh, the God of Enoch, the God of Noah, the God of Abraham, and the God of Isaac. But here He is no longer just the God of individuals, but El-Bethel, the God of the house of God. In Hebrew, "El" means God. In the title El-Bethel this Hebrew word for God is used twice, at both the beginning and the ending of this title. In a sense, the God of the house of God is double. We must admit that we do not yet have much experience of this. But we thank the Lord that after coming into the church life, we have had some experience of God's being God to us as a corporate body. In the church life, we do experience God corporately and not only individually. We all can testify that the God we experience in the church life is much richer and sweeter than the God we experience in our individual life. This is why we like to spend more time in the church life. Individually, we can experience the God of Abraham or the God of Isaac, but we cannot experience God as the God of Bethel. We can only experience the God of the house of God in the church life. If many years ago you had been told about the God of the corporate body, it would have sounded like a foreign language to you. But today this is not foreign to us. We are familiar with this experience and we appreciate it much more than our individual experience of God.

This does not mean, however, that there is not the aspect of experiencing God in an individual way. Even today, there is still this aspect. Never forget that the truths in the Bible have two aspects. This is also true of the experience of God, for the experience of God has a corporate aspect as well as an individual aspect. Many Christians today either have no experience of God or have just the individual experience of God. They lack the experience of God in a corporate way. But in meeting after meeting of the church life, we experience God in a corporate way.

At this point, I need to speak an honest word to some of you. Although you meet with us week after week, you do not have the corporate experience of God. For instance, you pray daily in your private life, but you never pray in the church meetings. In the meetings, you are observers, like a spectator at a ball game. You watch others play, but you yourselves do not play. You never participate in the meetings. Furthermore, some of you criticize those who do participate, saying that they are too bold or too quick. But what about you? Are you here to be critics, spectators, or to participate in the church life? This indicates that some among us do not appreciate the experience of God in a corporate way. Some of us still do not pray in the meetings. If you were asked to pray, you would always excuse yourselves. This reveals that you consider others as the priests and yourselves as the common people. By doing this you establish a clergy-laity hierarchy. In the eyes of God, this is heretical. We all must pray to overthrow this clergy-laity system.

According to my registration, the prayer meeting in Anaheim is better than that in any other church. I have visited nearly all the churches and I can testify that the prayer meeting in Anaheim is the best. The reason is that there is no clergy or laity in our prayer meeting. Although many pray, no one completes a prayer by himself. Rather, it may take many of us to finish one prayer. In the old, traditional way, when someone prayed, he not only finished one prayer but perhaps two or three other prayers at the same time. Either people did not pray at all, or they would pray several prayers in succession. But in Anaheim after someone prays a short sentence, someone else will follow him. In this way, many function together to offer one prayer. This is the experience of El-Bethel, the corporate experience of God.

Genesis 35 is a radical turn from the individual experience of God to the corporate experience of God. Before this chapter, El-Bethel is not mentioned. Elohim was revealed in chapter one, and Jehovah was revealed in chapter two. Later, God told Jacob that He was the God of Abraham and the God of Isaac. But, as we have pointed out, in chapter thirty-five we see a new divine title—El-Bethel, God of the house of God.

Elsewhere in this message we shall see the significance of God's telling Jacob that his name was no longer Jacob but Israel. God said to Jacob, "Israel shall be thy name" (v. 10), and Jacob seemed to say to God, "Your name is El-Bethel." Who are you today—Jacob or Israel? What does Israel mean? To answer that it means a wrestler of God is too doctrinal. Israel is the church people, and El-Bethel is the church life. We are the church people in the church life. This is not doctrine; it is experience. The church people are a people filled with God, and the church life is a corporate life of God. The church people are a people filled with God living together to enjoy God and to express Him. This is Israel in El-Bethel.

a) Jacob's Altar

At Bethel, Jacob built an altar (vv. 6-7). Jacob's experience of the altar was progressive. When he saw the vision at Bethel (28:18-19), he did not erect an altar. Although he did an excellent job of interpreting his dream, he only set up a pillar. During the years at Padan-aram, Jacob did not build an altar on which to offer something to God. Instead, he employed many gimmicks to supplant Laban. After leaving Padan-aram, Jacob firstly returned to the eastern part of Jordan to Succoth (33:17). In 33:17 and 18 the Bible does not say that Succoth is in "the land of Canaan," as it does with Shechem. At Succoth, Jacob built a house for himself and booths for his cattle, but he did not erect an altar for God. This reveals that he cared for himself and for his cattle, but that he did not care for God. Eventually, Jacob left Succoth and journeyed to Shechem in the land of Canaan, where he pitched his tent and erected an altar (33:18-20). Jacob called that altar "El-elohe-Israel," which means the God of Israel. This altar was built to the God of Jacob's individual, personal experience. In calling the altar El-elohe-Israel, he was actually calling it the God of himself. Many Christians are like this. They seek spiritual experiences for themselves individualistically. They have learned how to experience Christ and how to trust in God individualistically. God is not El-Bethel to them; He is El-elohe-Israel. But few Christians care for God's being the God of the house of God. On the contrary, nearly all Christian seekers care for God's being their God. Some of them might say, "Was not God the God of Abraham, the God of Isaac, and the God of Jacob? What is wrong with saying that God is my God? Oh, this wonderful God is my God!" Perhaps their book of Genesis does not have more than thirty chapters. They must proceed to chapter thirty-five and see that God is no longer merely the God of individuals, but the God of the house of God.

At Bethel in chapter twenty-eight, in Padan-aram, and in Succoth, Jacob had no altar. In Shechem he did build an altar. Although it was good to build an altar in Shechem, this altar was not built at the house of God; it was not built in the church life. Rather, it was erected at a place somewhat removed from the church life. If you consult a map, you will see that Shechem was not too far from Bethel. The word Shechem means shoulder, signifying strength. When Jacob came to Shechem, he was strengthened, for Shechem was a place of strengthening. Likewise, when we come to our "Shechem," we also are strengthened. Nearly all the revivals in today's Christianity take place in "Shechem." These revivals merely strengthen people. Many Christians need a "Shechem," a revival, once a year to strengthen them. No revivalists care for the church life. They are only concerned with strengthening people to go on in the Christian life. Nothing related to the church is covered by them.

The altar built at Shechem was called El-elohe-Israel, by the name of God as related to an individual, not El-Bethel, by the name of God as related to a corporate body. Some may say, "Isn't it good to be strengthened at Shechem?" But look at what happened to Jacob in chapter thirty-four. After he had settled down in Shechem, trouble came to him. He had a tent for his dwelling and an altar on which to sacrifice something to God. Although Jacob might have been satisfied, God was not. Thus, the experience of chapter thirty-four was necessary. Trouble came, and this trouble caused Jacob to lose his peace. Following this, in 35:1, God could say, "Arise, go up to Bethel and dwell there: and make there an altar unto God."

God seemed to be telling Jacob, "I don't want you to stay in Shechem. It is not adequate merely to be strengthened in the Christian life. A strengthened life can never satisfy Me. I desire the church life. I don't want strength—I want the house of God. I don't want you to remain in Shechem, but to go up to Bethel." After Jacob arrived at Bethel, he made an altar and called it El-Bethel.

Jacob's experience of the altar was a gradual progression. There was no altar in Padan-aram or in Succoth. The altar in Shechem was erected to the God of his individual experience; it was not an altar for the experience of God in a corporate way. The individual experience of God is good, but it is insufficient. We need to go on from the individual experience to the corporate experience.

An altar is for consecration. Probably all of you have consecrated yourselves to the Lord. But where was that consecration—at Shechem or at Bethel? Was that an experience of El-clohe-Israel or of El-Bethel? Before I came into the church life I had consecrated myself more than once. But the consecration I made after coming into the church life was much higher than any previous consecration. My consecration before the church life was only for myself. It was for me to be holy, spiritual, victorious, and acceptable to God. But my consecration after coming into the church life was different. When you live individualistically, you do not need very much consecration. After you get married, however, you find that your spouse is a troublemaker and that you need to consecrate yourself for this new situation. You may say to the Lord, "Lord, before getting married, I consecrated myself to You to be holy, spiritual, and victorious. Now that I am married I must consecrate myself to You for this. I like the windows opened, but my wife wants them closed. I need a consecration to match this situation." This consecration is new and different. Later, you have children, and this requires a further consecration. When you come into the church life, you not only have one troublemaker but hundreds of them. Many are afraid to come to Anaheim, thinking that it is too large and that the elders here are so strong and straight. They prefer to go to a smaller locality. This indicates that when we come into the church life we need a greater and greater consecration. When you get married, you need a consecration; when you have children, you need a greater consecration; and when you come into the church life, especially to the church in Anaheim, you need the greatest consecration. Without the topmost consecration, you could not bear the church life in Anaheim. You may say to yourself, "Oh, how difficult it is here in Anaheim! There are 'policemen' everywhere. I simply cannot adapt to this situation." Since you cannot adjust to it, you must build an altar to match it. As we all know, in front of the temple there was an altar, and no one could enter into the temple without first lingering at the altar. You must stop at the altar and offer yourself, putting yourself on the altar to be slaughtered. Then, after you have been resurrected, you will be free to enter into the temple.

What is the significance of an altar? An altar is for slaughter. Some have said, "The church life is good, but I cannot stand those leading brothers." Others have said, "I appreciate the church life, but I cannot bear the leading sisters. They are too holy. Their holiness slaughters me." Where then should you go—back to Shechem or Padan-aram? You have no alternative except to climb on the altar at Bethel and be slaughtered. The altar in Shechem is an individual altar, but the altar in El-Bethel is a corporate altar. This is the altar of the house of God, and you must present yourself upon it for the house of God. I have done this many times and, years ago, I was slaughtered. Now, no one can offend me. You cannot offend anyone who has been slaughtered. If you do not take in this word and build an altar at El-Bethel, you will not remain in the church forever. One day, you will either walk away or become indifferent. When you are happy, you will come to the meetings, but when you are unhappy, you will not come. It seems that the church is the church, that you are you, and that you and the church have nothing to do with each other. If you do not become indifferent, you will leave because you have been offended. The church is full of offenders. I was slaughtered long ago for the church life in mainland China. Thus, none of you can slaughter me anymore. I cannot be offended by you. This is the experience of the altar built at

Bethel. If you can still be offended, it means that, although you may have an altar in Shechem, you do not have an altar in Bethel. To have an altar in Bethel means to have a consecration for the church life. You need to purposely and specifically offer yourself to the Lord for the church life. If you do this, you will never be offended. Rather, you will be prepared for trials, tests, and sufferings. We all need such an altar. This is the experience at Bethel, the experience of the church life.

If you read chapters twenty-eight through thirty-five again, paying attention to this matter of the altar, you will notice the progression from no altar to the highest altar, the altar at El-Bethel. We need a definite, specific consecration for the church life. We need to say, "Lord, now I would make a thorough and specific consecration to You, not that I might be holy, spiritual, or victorious, but that I might experience Your house and remain in it." In 1 Timothy 3:15 Paul said to Timothy, "If I delay, that you may know how one ought to conduct himself in the house of God, which is the church of the living God." We need to experience God in His house and to behave in the house of God. This requires a definite consecration and a special altar. The common, ordinary altar that we experienced in the past will not be adequate for this. We all need the topmost consecration at the altar in Bethel.

In the past centuries, a number of books have been put out by Christian teachers on the subject of consecration. But, as far as I know, none of them tells Christians to consecrate themselves for the house of God. Mrs. Hannah W. Smith's famous book, *The Christian's Secret of a Happy Life,* places great stress on the matter of consecration, but it is only for a happy Christian life. She even considers consecration to be a secret of the happy Christian life, but she says nothing for the church life. The Keswick Convention, with which Mrs. Smith had much to do, also emphasized consecration. Actually, in the early days, the messages given at the Keswick Convention were focused on consecration. However, as far as I know, nothing was mentioned regarding consecration for the church life. In nearly every revival in Christianity consecration is stressed, but one can hardly hear of the consecration for the house of God. Because Christians have not seen the church life, all their altars are, at best, built in "Shechem." But in the Lord's recovery today we must build our altar at Bethel. We need the topmost consecration for the church life to fulfill God's eternal purpose and to satisfy His heart's desire.

b) God's Appearing

Jacob also experienced a progressive advancement in the matter of God's appearing. God appeared to him in a dream in chapter twenty-eight, but that appearing was not substantial. Nothing that we see in a dream is substantial. It may be correct, but it is not concrete. Nebuchadnezzar saw a great image of a human body in a dream (Dan. 2:31), but that image was not as substantial as a real human body, and the two iron legs in the dream were not as solid as the two sections of the Roman Empire. While Nebuchadnezzar beheld those things in a dream, he had no experience of them. Likewise, although Jacob experienced God's appearing in his dream, in El-Bethel he solidly experienced God's appearing. The Lord spoke to Jacob when he was in Padan-aram (31:3), but that was not a solid appearing of the Lord. In 35:1, the Lord also spoke to him, but that also was not a solid appearing. Only in El-Bethel did Jacob experience God's appearing in a substantial way. This is the progress in Jacob's experience of God's appearing.

Many of us can testify that before entering into the church life we had some experience of God's appearing. God did appear to us, but that appearing was not solid. But after coming to the church life and being in it for a time, we can testify that here God's appearing is not only real but also solid. If anyone would leave the church life after remaining in it for a time, he could never deny that while he was in the church life he had experienced the appearing of God in a solid way. Before we came into the church life, the appearing of God was rather vague. But the appearing of God in the church is always substantial. It is so concrete that it seems that we can almost touch it. The best experience of God's appearing is only in the church.

c) God's Blessing

There is also a progression in God's blessing. In the vision in Bethel (28:13-15), in Padan-aram, and in Shechem (31:3; 35:1), Jacob was not given God's blessing. God did bless Jacob in Peniel, but there He did not bless him solidly (32:29). Jacob was not given God's substantial blessing because he was not yet in the place where God intended him to be. At Peniel, we are told that God blessed Jacob, but we are not told in what way He blessed him. However, in chapter thirty-five, at Bethel, the blessing is very solid. There, God blessed Jacob, saying, "I am God, all-sufficient: be fruitful and multiply; a nation and a company of nations shall be of thee, and kings shall come out of thy loins; and the land which I gave Abraham and Isaac, to thee I will give it, and to thy seed after thee will I give the land" (vv. 11-12, Heb.). These are the solid items of God's blessing in Bethel.

d) Jacob's Experience of His New Name

In Bethel, Jacob experienced his new name. His name had been changed at Peniel (32:28, 30), but he experienced his new name at Bethel (35:10). At Bethel, Jacob's entire being was changed and he became a new person—Israel. No matter how good we were as Christians before we came into the church life, we were not new. But after we came into the church life, something within demanded us to be new. We had to be a new husband, a new parent, a new child. We all experience this inward demanding daily. We realize that, from now on, we must be another person. This is the experience of transformation.

The church life is a transforming life. In the church, everyone is under the process of renewal. We are being renewed day by day (Rom. 12:2; 2 Cor. 4:16). We are not being corrected, for that means nothing, but we are being renewed. The church is altogether a new man (Eph. 2:15), and the church life is the life of the transformed Israel. It is a new life with a new person and a new being. Here, in Bethel, we experience the new life, which is God in Christ. Here, in the church life, we are becoming newer every day. The longer we stay in the proper church life, the newer we become. Your chronological age may get older, but your being becomes newer. All the elderly brothers and sisters must become newer, quicker, stronger, and fresher. In their sharing they need to be louder and faster than the young people.

I expect that all the points in this message will become your practical experience. In the church life, we need the highest consecration, the consecration for the house of God, not for individual enrichment. If we have this, then we shall have God's appearing in a substantial way and enjoy His full blessing. Then we shall daily become newer and newer. This is the experience at Bethel, the experience of the church life.

LIFE-STUDY OF GENESIS

MESSAGE EIGHTY-ONE

BEING TRANSFORMED

(4)

We need to consider further the experience at Bethel. In this message we come to God's promise.

e) God's Promise

We may be quite familiar with the term promise. In this portion of the Word, however, God's promise is not common. The God who gives the promise in chapter thirty-five is God all-sufficient (v. 11, Heb.). We need to give attention to the revelation of God's titles in the book of Genesis. In chapter one, God is only revealed as Elohim, and in chapter two we see the title Jehovah (rendered Lord in the King James Version). Elohim is God's title as Creator in relation to His creation, and Jehovah is His title in His relationship with man, revealing how God is related to man. The title the all-sufficient God, or God all-sufficient, is not revealed until 17:1, where God said to Abraham, "I am the all-sufficient God; walk before me and be thou perfect" (Heb.). In the past, we did not adequately realize the significance of this title. We thought that it simply meant that God was everything to us. Undoubtedly, it is correct to say that God's all-sufficiency means that He is everything to us. But for what purpose is this title of God revealed? I have given a number of messages in the past on this title of God, telling people that it denotes that God is rich and that He is our all-sufficient supply. He is everything to supply all our need. In a sense, this was right. God is all-sufficient in order to supply us. But for what does He supply us? Does He supply us merely in order that we might be saved or be spiritual? No. If we would see the purpose for God's being the all-sufficient One, we need to read Genesis 35 and compare it with Genesis 17.

The purpose of God's revealing Himself as the all-sufficient God is for His building. Just as Elohim is for God's creation, so the all-sufficient God is for God's building. Do not understand the Holy Word by your imagination. Understand the Bible by the Bible itself, by comparing one portion of the Word with another. How do we know that Elohim is for God's creation? All Bible students agree that the first mention of an item in the Bible establishes a principle for that particular thing. The first mention of Elohim is in Genesis 1. In this chapter, God is revealed for His creation. Therefore, this establishes the principle that Elohim basically denotes the creating God, God the Creator.

Genesis 17:1, the first mention of the title the all-sufficient God, El-Shaddai, clearly reveals the significance of this title. Prior to that time, Abraham had been called by God for the purpose of becoming the father of so many of God's called ones. God did not intend that Abraham fulfill this by the exercise of his natural strength, and God did not give Abraham a child until his natural strength had been exhausted. Abraham, however, neither understood God adequately, nor had faith in Him for this. Instead, he followed his wife's proposal that he bring forth a child by using his natural strength with a concubine. God was offended by this and did not speak to Abraham for thirteen years. Do not think that God cannot be offended, or that He will always be patient with you. We are nowhere told in the Bible that God is all-patient. In Abraham's case, God was offended, not by sin, but by the exercise of Abraham's natural strength. In God's economy, nothing offends Him more than your exercise of your natural strength. Whenever a called one of God uses his natural strength to do something for the accomplishment of God's purpose, God will be offended. In a sense, using your natural strength is an insult to God. God does not need your help. To exercise your natural strength means that you are capable of helping God. This indicates that God is not sufficient and that He needs you to assist Him. When God spoke to Abraham again after an interval of thirteen years, He said,

"I am the all-sufficient God." If you read this chapter carefully, you will see that God's being all-sufficient is for us to produce the materials for His house.

Genesis 17 and 35 correspond to each other in at least three ways. Firstly, both chapters reveal that God is all-sufficient. God revealed this divine title to both Abraham and Jacob. Secondly, in both chapters a change of name occurs. Abraham's name was changed from Abram to Abraham, and Jacob's name was changed from Jacob to Israel. In spiritual life, the change of name signifies transformation, not merely the change of label. You may say, "Witness Lee, you have done something wrong. From now on, you are not Witness Lee but Charles Ford." This change of label means nothing. According to the Bible, to change your name is to change your being. Formerly, you were Abram; now you are Abraham. Previously, you were a supplanting Jacob; now you are Israel, the wrestler of God. This is the change, not of a label, but of your being, of your constitution. Hence, chapter seventeen speaks of the transformation of Abraham and chapter thirty-five speaks of the transformation of Jacob.

Thirdly, in both chapters we have God's promise. God's promise to Abraham is repeated in His promise to Jacob. God's promise to Jacob in chapter twenty-eight was indefinite. In 28:14 God said, "Thy seed shall be as the dust of the earth." If I had been Jacob, I would have said, "Lord, I don't want my descendants to be dust. Instead of millions of particles of dust, I would rather have a few kings." Although God's promise in chapter twenty-eight speaks of dust, His promise in chapter thirty-five speaks of kings and nations (v. 11). A nation denotes a kingdom. God's promise in 35:11 is a repetition of His promise in 17:6. In both instances, He promised that nations and kings would come forth. In Jacob's dream at Bethel, God told him that his seed would be as dust. But now, in the actual experience at Bethel in chapter thirty-five, God's promise has advanced. Here, there is no mention of dust. Instead of dust there are nations with kings. The focus of the promise in this chapter is to be fruitful and multiply to bring forth nations with kings. Thus, Genesis 17 and 35 correspond to each other in three respects: in the revelation of the divine title, the all-sufficient God; in the changing of human names; and in the promise of multiplication for bringing forth nations with kings.

Now we can see the purpose of the title the all-sufficient God. The all-sufficient God is for the building of God's house. We all need to take in this word. The all-sufficient God is for the building of Bethel. God is all-sufficient for the church life, for the building of His house on earth. You cannot experience the all-sufficient God in an individualistic way. In order to experience the all-sufficient God, you must be in Bethel, in the house of God, in the church life.

This truth is proved by our experience. Before we came to the church life, many of us had some experience of God. But as we all can testify, we did not experience God as the all-sufficient One. Although I experienced God in various aspects, I did not experience Him as the all-sufficient One until I came into the church life. But after being in the church life for many years, I can say, "Hallelujah, what an experience of the all-sufficient God I have in the church life!" God is too all-sufficient to be experienced by just a few individual believers. As individuals, we are too limited. God's all-sufficiency requires a corporate body. We need the house in order to experience this aspect of Him.

Recently, we had a marvelous prayer meeting here in Anaheim. I believe that that meeting will stand as a memorial for eternity. All the utterances in the prayers were unique. In our prayers we prayed about the travailing woman and about the prevailing, victorious man-child. It was wonderful! We could never have prayer like this alone in our rooms; we must be in the church. Any local saints who missed that prayer meeting certainly missed a great deal. This is an experience, not of Elohim or of Jehovah, but of the all-sufficient God. In that prayer meeting I was above the third heaven enjoying the all-sufficient God. Only in the church life is it possible to realize the all-sufficiency of our God.

When I hear of the opposition from our critics, I do not feel hateful toward them; rather, I feel full of pity. How much they are missing! Their traditional religion is frustrating them and keeping them from God's up-to-date move. What an all-sufficient God we are experiencing in His present move! This is not a teaching or a doctrinal understanding; it is our experience of God in the church life. The all-sufficient God is revealed for the building of Bethel and He is experienced in the church life.

The New Testament interpretation of the Old Testament term "the house of God" is "the church." In 1 Timothy 3:15 Paul said, "But if I delay, that you may know how one ought to conduct himself in the house of God, which is the church of the living God, the pillar and base of the truth." For us today, Bethel is not history; it is the church of the living God. The Bethel in the Old Testament is a type of the practical experience of the church life. What poverty there is in today's Christianity! Most Christians think of Bethel as past history. They do not realize that the church life today is Bethel. The reason that they do not understand this is that they do not have the church life. Praise the Lord that in the Lord's recovery we have the church life!

In the church life, our experience of the all-sufficient God is increasing day by day and even minute by minute. Our church life in Anaheim has greatly increased in the last two years. If you compare January, 1977 with January, 1975, you will see the difference. Surely, 1977 will be a great year in the Lord's recovery. In October of this year there will be in Taipei an international conference of the churches. Only the Lord knows what will happen at that time, or even next week. I believe that some very significant things are about to happen. The church life is marching on; it is advancing day and night. Many of us can testify that the church life has advanced since this afternoon. Hallelujah, the all-sufficient God is for the church life, today's Bethel!

(1) Not in Padan-aram

In Padan-aram, God did not give a promise to Jacob (31:3). Why did God not give him a promise there? It certainly was not because God changes, for God never changes. No promise was given to Jacob in Padan-aram because that was not the proper place. In Padan-aram, Jacob was not in the right position to receive God's promise. If we would receive God's promise, we must be in the proper place. I say strongly that many things can only be received in the church life. Outside of the church life, you do not have the position to receive these things.

(2) Not in Succoth or in Shechem

Eventually, Jacob left Padan-aram and journeyed to Succoth, which means "booths" (33:17). In Succoth, which was on the border of the good land, Jacob built a house for himself and booths for his cattle, but he did not erect an altar for God. Later, Jacob traveled from Succoth to Shechem. We have seen that in Shechem he built an altar. But this altar was built at the place of his own satisfaction, not at the place of God's satisfaction. Thus, God changed Jacob's circumstances that he might be stirred up and receive the charge to arise and go up to Bethel. Neither in Succoth nor in Shechem did Jacob receive God's promise.

(3) Only in Bethel

Only in Bethel did God give His promise to Jacob (35:11-12). The promise in chapter thirty-five is more solid than the promise given to Jacob in the dream (28:13-14). Before we came to the church life, we never had a solid promise given to us by God. The most solid promises are always given in the church life. Our experience after coming into the church life is that nearly every day is a day of promise. This means that every day is full of expectations. Outside the church, we had no hope. Did you have hope before coming into the church life? No, we only had disappointment and discouragement. But now, in the church life, everything is so definite and meaningful. Morning, noon, and night we have hope. All these hopes are the promises we are receiving day after day.

All the promises given by God and received by us in the church life are for God's building. They are not for our little cottage or hut. In the past, some of us desired to build a little cottage of holiness, and some of the sisters expected to build the little hut of a good married life. Many wives who have not found married life enjoyable have sought to find a happy married life in Christianity. Even after coming into the church life, many sisters still have deep within them the hope of finding in the church the happy married life they have been seeking. Their intention is not for the building up of the house of God; it is to build the little hut of their married life. But the experience of many of us is this: when we were endeavoring to build a little hut for ourselves, God blew upon it. In my experience years ago, God firstly blew away the roof and then the walls. After that, my hut was gone. But do not think that all the church people are miserable because the hut of their married life has been demolished. We have a much better married life, not in our little hut, but in the house of God. Today, in the church life, I can testify and boast to the enemy concerning the wonderful married life I have in the church. If you did not have the church life, what a miserable married life you would have! When we tried to build a little hut for ourselves, we were unsuccessful. But when we brought our married life into the church, we found ourselves in a mansion. Praise the Lord that we are here for the house of God!

Before I came into the church life, I also attempted to build a little house of patience. As many of you know, I am a quick person. It takes a great deal of energy for a fast person to be patient. I even hate to get a busy signal when I dial the telephone. Realizing as a young man that I lacked patience, I attempted to build a little house of patience. I also did my best to build houses of holiness and victory. I wanted very much to be victorious over my temper. A fast person is impatient, and impatience causes us to lose our temper. I was quite aware that I was impatient, unholy, and defeated. Although I tried to build houses of patience, holiness, and victory, I was not successful in building even one of them. When I came into the church life, I did not immediately forget these houses. Rather, I still attempted to build them. But one day I saw that it was foolish to build these small houses, for I already had one large house—the church life. As long as we are in the church life, patience, holiness, and victory are ours.

Let me share with you something I have experienced many times. When I was on the verge of losing my temper, I thought about the church, and immediately my temper disappeared.

Perhaps I said to myself, "I am about to lose my temper with the elders." But, by the Lord's mercy, I thought about the church, and my temper vanished. There is not always the need to even experience the church life. Even a thought about the church life can quell our temper. You may say, "Brother Lee, this is superstitious. How can a little thought about the church life take away your temper?" I cannot explain this, but I know that I have experienced that even a thought about the church can make you victorious. If you actually live in the church life, what holiness and victory you will have! When you get into the New Jerusalem, will you still be seeking holiness, humility, and patience? No, when you get into the New Jerusalem, all this vocabulary will be terminated. There will be no patience, just God Himself as the all-sufficient God. In the church life we have a miniature of the New Jerusalem today. No other Christians experience holiness as much as we do. We are not building our cottages and huts. We are only for the unique building—the house of God. This house is a mutual habitation. Both we and God abide here. Praise the Lord that we are now in the church life experiencing God in a corporate way!

The promise in 35:11, given by the all-sufficient God, is mainly for us to be fruitful and multiply. It seems that this resembles gospel preaching. Although there may be some similarity between this promise and gospel preaching, the preaching of the gospel today is a form of fruit-bearing. While preaching the gospel might be an outward activity, bearing fruit is an inward overflow of life. To be fruitful and to multiply means to bring forth children, to produce something out of the riches of your inner life. This can only happen through the overflow of the rich inner life.

Suppose we were all "monkeys" and God said, "Monkeys, be fruitful." If this were the case, a great many "monkeys" would be brought forth. Certainly, God does not desire this kind of multiplication. God wants the multiplication of Israel, not of Jacob. As we have seen, the name Israel has the Hebrew letters for God—El—in it. Our multiplication must be the multiplication of God. The "monkey" multiplication is not the multiplication of God because a "monkey" does not have the essence, the element, of God in it. It lacks the "El." But Israel contains some part of God. We need to be transformed for multiplication. Before Abram became Abraham, God never told him to be fruitful. If God had spoken this word before Abram had become Abraham, the natural man, not the transformed one, would have been multiplied. Only after Abraham had been circumcised and had experienced the changing of name did God promise to make him "exceeding fruitful" (17:6). It is the same with Jacob. In chapter twenty-eight, God did not promise Jacob that he would be fruitful and multiply. There, He only said that Jacob's seed would be as dust. But it is different in chapter thirty-five. Here, God promised Israel that he would be fruitful and multiply and that nations with kings would come out of him. This is not the multiplication of "monkeys," but of Israels.

In their gospel preaching, many Christians have brought forth "monkeys," which are not good for the church life. Do you want to have a multiplication of "monkeys"? No. We must have the multiplication of Israels. In order to have this, we need to be transformed from Jacob into Israel because only Israel can bring forth Israel. Hence, the promise in this chapter is based upon the fact of Jacob's being transformed. This also is for the building of God's house.

Although I brought some people to the Lord before I came into the church life, none of them came into the church life. I brought them into Christianity, but, as hard as I tried, I could not bring them into the church life. But after I entered into the church life, hundreds of others who were brought to the Lord in my early preaching not only came to salvation, but also entered into the church life. You may say, "Brother Lee, before you came into the church life, you were Jacob, and, thus, you brought forth other Jacobs." That is right. But after I came into the church life and experienced transformation, nearly all those whom I brought to the Lord became the material for the building of the local church life, for the building of the house of God. There is a great difference between gospel preaching and this kind of multiplication. We are not merely preaching the gospel by carrying on certain outward activities; we are living the church life to bring forth the proper fruit for the church life.

Notice that verse 11 does not say that this multiplication is for Bethel. Rather, it indicates that it is for nations with kings. This reveals, or at least implies, that the proper church life must be the kingdom. The result of our multiplication must be the church life, and this church life must be the kingdom.

There is a problem with interpreting the phrase "a company of nations" in verse 11. How many nations actually came out of Jacob? Only the nation of Israel issued from him. However, in Hebrew the word translated "company" means a multitude. Furthermore, in 17:5 Abraham is called the "father of a multitude of nations" (Heb.). What are the many nations of which Abraham is the father? I do not believe that God counts the Arab nations because they are the descendants of Ishmael. Only one nation, the nation of Israel, has come out of Abraham. We need the whole Bible to develop any of the seeds found in the book of Genesis. Undoubtedly, Israel was a nation, a kingdom. The church, the millennium, and the New Jerusalem in eternity will also be kingdoms.

Even today, the church life must be a nation, a kingdom. Our multiplication must result in nations. This means that whatever fruit we bear must issue in the church life, which will be a genuine kingdom of God with kings. We are not only here for the church life, but also for the kingdom. For the church we do not need much discipline, but for the kingdom we need considerable discipline.

At the end of the Gospel of Mark, the Lord said to His disciples, "Go into all the world and preach the gospel" (Mark 16:15), and in the conclusion of Luke it is written, "That repentance for forgiveness of sins should be proclaimed in His name to all the nations" (Luke 24:47). But in Matthew 28:19, the Lord said, "Go therefore and disciple all the nations." The Gospel of Matthew is concerned with the kingdom, and in this Gospel the church life today is the kingdom. Matthew 16:18-19 indicates this: "On this rock I will build My church, and the gates of Hades shall not prevail against it. I will give to you the keys of the kingdom of the heavens." In these verses the words church and kingdom are interchangeable. This reveals that the church is the kingdom and that the kingdom is the church. The church life today must be the kingdom. Because in Christianity there is no kingdom, it is true to say that in Christianity there is not the proper church. In Christianity there is no discipleship, no discipline. We must bear the fruit who will be genuine disciples, those who will come under the divine discipline so that the church life might truly be the kingdom. In the church life today, there is the need of discipline. If we do not accept this discipline today, how can we expect to reign during the kingdom age? If you have never been disciplined under God's authority, you will not know how to rule over the nations. The church life is a preparation for the kingdom, and in it we are now being disciplined to be Christ's co-kings.

LIFE-STUDY OF GENESIS

MESSAGE EIGHTY-TWO

BEING TRANSFORMED

(5)

f) Jacob's Doing

(1) Building a Pillar

In this message we shall still dwell on the experience at Bethel. In 35:14, at Bethel Jacob eventually set up a pillar of stone as he did after having the dream when he was at Bethel the first time (28:18). There, this pillar of stone was called the house of God (28:22). If Jacob had not called this pillar the house of God, we would never realize that the pillar of stone was for the building of God's house. We would think that it was simply a mass of rock. But now we know that this stone can become a house. This indicates that the pillar will become a building, the house of God.

In the book of Genesis, there are two kinds of pillars—the pillar of stone (28:18; 35:14) and the pillar of salt (19:26). Which kind of pillar do you want to be? Certainly, we all want to be pillars of stone. The pillar of stone indicates building in strength. Solomon set up two pillars in the porch of the temple (1 Kings 7:21). The first pillar was named Jachin, which means, "He shall establish," and the second was named Boaz, which means, "In it is strength." The pillar of stone not only indicates building, but building in strength. The pillar of salt indicates shame, for a pillar of salt is useless for God's purpose. Lot's wife, who was one of God's called people, became a pillar of shame. She should have been building material, but due to her degradation she became shameful material.

During the course of this life-study, we have seen again and again that nearly everything in this book is a seed of the truth that is developed in the following books of the Bible. The way to study Genesis is to trace all its points in the subsequent books of the Bible. The way to study the book of Revelation is just the opposite. If you would understand Revelation, you must trace its points backward in the foregoing books. In this message we need to follow the development of the seed of the pillar.

(a) A General Sketch

aa. For the Temple

After Solomon built the temple, he purposely added the two pillars. According to our natural concept, we would think that Solomon should firstly have built the pillars and then the temple. But it was after he had built the temple that he proceeded to build two pillars and to place them in front of the temple (1 Kings 7:15-22). If we could have seen that temple, our eyes would have firstly attended, not to the temple itself, but to these two pillars. The size of these pillars is seemingly out of proportion to the size of the temple. The disproportionate size of the pillars is significant. It indicates that the two pillars in the temple are like a huge signboard. Today, when we approach a certain building, there is a sign designating what that building is. Likewise, in front of the temple were two pillars which said, "God shall establish," and, "In it is strength." These two pillars declare to the whole universe, including mankind, Satan, and all the fallen angels, that the Lord establishes and that strength is in the building. The Bible emphatically says that the first pillar is called Jachin and the second Boaz. We have pointed out that the name Jachin means, "He shall establish" and that the name Boaz means, "In it is strength." This reveals clearly that the building of God's house is altogether dependent on the pillar. This is the reason that Jacob did not build the house of God, but only set up a pillar.

In chapter twenty-eight, Jacob was still a supplanter. Nevertheless, this supplanter received both the vision and the interpretation of the vision. He interpreted his vision, his dream, by setting up a pillar and calling it God's house. This interpretation was much better than Daniel's interpretation of Nebuchadnezzar's dreams. Daniel merely interpreted; he did not set up anything or take any action. Jacob, however, not only interpreted his dream verbally, saying, "This is the house of God"; he also set up a pillar and called it the house of God. How could Jacob, an unrepentant, unregenerated, and untransformed supplanter, have done such a wonderful thing? Nevertheless, he did it, and we all must say, "Thank you, Jacob, for opening the heavens that we might see the house of God."

For the building of God's house, the heavens were opened by a supplanter. I believe this because the Bible tells us so. I do not trust in my concept, for according to my concept, it would be impossible for a supplanter to do this. I could easily believe that a godly and pious person like Daniel, a man who prayed daily, could have interpreted a spiritual dream. But it seems neither fair nor logical for a supplanter to do this. But he did it spontaneously. This is absolutely a matter of grace. As Romans 9:11 indicates, it is "not of works, but of Him who calls." Romans 9:13 says, "Jacob I loved, but Esau I hated." Grace is not a matter of fairness. Do not question God, saying, "God, why do You hate Esau? To me Esau is better than Jacob. It is unfair for You to love Jacob and hate Esau." To this, God would reply, "I simply love Jacob and hate Esau. What do you have to say about this? When I hate, I have the position to hate, and when I love, I have the grace to love." Who are you—Esau or Jacob, a good man or a supplanter? We all must confess that we are Jacobs, heel-holders, supplanters. The church is filled with heel-holders. If you are not a heel-holder, you will miss God's grace. We are true heel-holders, but we are heel-holders in grace. No one can deny this. I can shout and declare, "Praise the Lord that I am a heel-holder in grace. Grace makes me different."

Although in chapter twenty-eight Jacob was a supplanter, by the time we come to chapter forty-eight we see that this supplanter has been thoroughly transformed into a man of God. This man of God is the pillar. In a sense, the house of God was built with this pillar. When you enter into the temple of God in the universe, the first thing you see is this God-man, this Israel standing before God's building. After Jacob was transformed into Israel, he stood in front of God's building as a signboard of God's house.

bb. For the Building of the Church

As we proceed to the New Testament, we see that the Lord Jesus came through incarnation. His incarnation was the erecting of a tabernacle (John 1:14). This tabernacle, which was erected that God might dwell among men, was a precursor of the temple. When you see a little boy, you know that a full-grown man is coming. Likewise, when you see the tabernacle, you realize that the temple is coming. As the tabernacle, Jesus was the indicator that God's temple was soon to appear. This is why the Lord changed the name of Simon, the representative of the first group of disciples, to Cephas, which means a stone (John 1:42). In Matthew 16:18, after Peter had answered the Lord's question, "Who do you say that I am?" by saying, "You are the Christ, the Son of the living God," the Lord Jesus responded, "You are a stone" (Gk.). The Lord seemed to be saying, "I am Christ, the rock, and you are a stone to be built upon Me for the building up of My church." In his first Epistle, Peter later said, "You yourselves also, as living stones, are being built up a spiritual house" (1 Pet. 2:5). Consider also the case of the Apostle Paul. Formerly, he was an opposer of God's building, doing everything possible to persecute, damage, and lay it waste. But as he was on his way to Damascus to persecute the church, he was caught by the Lord and became not only the material for the building, but also a wise masterbuilder (1 Cor. 3:10).

In Galatians 2:9 Paul said that James, Cephas, and John were reputed to be pillars. At that time, they were respected by the saints as pillars. The pillars in 1 Kings 7:21 refer to the building of the temple of God in the Old Testament, but the pillars in Galatians 2:9 refer to the building of God's house in the New Testament. Many Christians realize that Peter and John were disciples and apostles, but not many realize that they were also pillars. They were not only disciples discipled by the Lord and apostles who discipled, taught, and edified others; they were also pillars, signboards of God's building in the New Testament. If you came to Peter, John, and James, they would not declare doctrine or religion to you. Instead, just as the pillars in front of the temple did not declare religion, teachings, or commandments, but the temple, so they would declare the house of God. When anyone saw the two pillars in front of the temple, they immediately realized that the temple was there. Likewise, when we see Peter, James, and John, we realize that the building of God's house is there. Many Christians view things through colored glasses. When you speak to them of Peter, they simply think of him as an apostle. Do you have the concept that Peter is a pillar? For years, whenever I thought of Peter and John, I considered them as apostles, not as strong pillars. Recently, however, the Lord has revolutionized my concept. Now whenever I think of Peter, James, and John, I think of three large columns standing before me. When we see these columns, we do not think of religion or doctrine; we think of the house of God. These pillars stand in the universe to declare Bethel, God's temple.

cc. In the New Jerusalem

Do not think that in this matter of the pillars I am allegorizing the Bible. The letters G-o-d spell "God," and the letters d-o-g spell "dog." This is not allegorization; it is reading. God, who is the best typesetter, has printed some very clear words for our understanding. Firstly, in Genesis 19:26 He typeset a negative pillar, the pillar of salt. By mentioning this negative pillar, God is asking us whether we want to become a pillar of salt. In chapter twenty-eight, we have the pillar of stone, and in 1 Kings 7 we have the two pillars in front of the temple. In Galatians 2:9 pillars are mentioned again, this time with respect to the temple of God in the New Testament. In Revelation 3:12, the Lord again speaks of the pillar, saying, "He who overcomes, I will make him a pillar in the temple of My God." The pillar in this verse does not refer to the temple in either the Old Testament or the New Testament, but to the New Jerusalem in the coming kingdom and in eternity. The temple of God is in three stages, three dispensations: the Old Testament stage, the New Testament stage, and the stage in the kingdom and in eternity. First Kings 7 covers the Old Testament stage, Galatians 2:9 covers the New Testament stage, and Revelation 3:12 covers God's building in the kingdom age and in eternity. This is God's way of typesetting. We put G-o-d together and we read the word "God." Likewise, as we put 1 Kings 7:21, Galatians 2:9, and Revelation 3:12 together, we can say, "Now I understand why, in interpreting his vision of God's house, Bethel, Jacob set up a pillar. The pillar is an indicator, a signboard, a designation, of the house of God."

In 1 Kings 7:21 there were just two pillars, and in Galatians 2:9 there were only three pillars. How many pillars will there be in the coming age? The number will not be written by the Lord, but by you and me. No one knows how many pillars there will be. We can only say, "Whosoever will may be." Whosoever will may be a pillar in the temple of God. The door is wide open. Unlike certain outstanding universities who only accept a limited number of their applicants, there is no limitation to the number who desire to be and may become pillars in the temple of God in the coming age. The number, whether it be a thousand or a million, is open. If the number were limited to two, none of us would have an opportunity. It would be hopeless for us to be pillars. But the number is not limited—it is, "Whosoever will may be." Are you willing to be made a pillar? I am. What mercy the Lord has upon us!

Consider the size of the Holy of Holies in the tabernacle. It was a cube of ten cubits in each dimension (Exo. 26:8,16). The Holy of Holies in the temple was somewhat larger, being a cube of twenty cubits in each dimension (1 Kings 6:20). But consider how large the Holy of Holies in the coming New Jerusalem will be. The entire city, which is twelve thousand stadia in length, breadth, and height, (approximately 1,363 miles, about the distance from Los Angeles to Dallas) will be an enlarged Holy of Holies (Rev. 21:16). For the small Holy of Holies, two pillars were sufficient. But how many pillars will be needed for the enlarged Holy of Holies? The answer is, "Whosoever will may be." There is a place for you. If you would not occupy this place, there would be a vacancy in eternity.

I have been reading and studying the Bible for more

than fifty years. The Bible is too profound, and no one can understand it to the uttermost. I believe that what I am ministering to you in this message has been mined from the depths of this book. In the Old Testament, two pillars indicated the temple of God, and in the New Testament, three pillars declared God's building. But the pillars in the coming kingdom and in the New Jerusalem in eternity will be numberless. Today, whosoever will may be one of these pillars.

dd. The Need to Be in Bethel

Now we need to consider how to become a pillar. I believe that all of us, young and old alike, are eager to know this. If you would know how to be a pillar, you must consider five different places: the place of Lot's wife, who became a pillar of salt; the place where Jacob set up the pillar at Bethel; the place of Solomon, where he built the two pillars; the place of Peter, James, and John, who were pillars of the New Testament church; and the place of the church in Philadelphia, where we see that whosoever will may be a pillar. Is your position that of Lot's wife? To this question, you should certainly answer, "No!" But is your position that of Jacob, the two pillars in the temple, the three pillars in the New Testament, and that of the ones in Philadelphia in Revelation 3:12? To this, you must answer, "Yes," for your position must be in each of these four places. Firstly, you need to take the position of Jacob, then the position of Solomon's pillars, then the position of the three pillars, and finally the position of Philadelphia. If you would be a pillar in the coming New Jerusalem, you must escape the place of Lot's wife. As long as you stay with her, you cannot be a pillar of stone. Recall the Lord's warning in Luke 17:32: "Remember Lot's wife." Today, many Christians are in the position of Lot's wife. This is even true of some of us. It seems that many do not care whether they become a pillar of salt or a pillar of stone. But you must care. If you do not care now, you will care someday. Someday, you will not only repent of your indifference, but also regret it.

After we have escaped the position of Lot's wife, we must come to Bethel. During the past fifty years, we have been burdened by God with Bethel. We simply cannot keep away from the church. We have been condemned for this and people have said that we are too extreme regarding the church. They accuse us of being too much for the church and of not caring for gospel preaching, Bible teaching, or other types of Christian work. My answer to this accusation is this: "I am not yet enough for the church. I am not 'crazy' enough for the church." Do not think that this is my concept. If you read your New Testament, you will see that the pillars—Peter, James, John, as well as Paul—were "crazy" for God's building. Through the years, many have argued with me, saying, "As long as we preach the gospel, win souls, teach people the Bible, and help them to love the Lord, isn't this good enough?" My answer is, "Where is the church? In Matthew 16:18 the Lord Jesus said, 'I will build My church.' Where is this builded church? Can the Lord's word fail to be fulfilled? Where, with whom, and by what way will He build His church?" Now is the time for the building of the church. Here and now, with us, the Lord is building His church. Many Christians devote their attention to the study of prophecy. The greatest prophecy is the Lord's word in Matthew 16:18—"I will build My church." Do not be occupied with Israel, Antichrist, the restored Roman Empire, or the ten horns. Rather, you must devote your full attention to the Lord's declaration in Matthew 16:18. Throughout the centuries, and even today, this church has not yet been built up. Because of this, we are burdened about the church.

If you would be a pillar of stone, you must be in Bethel. Bethel is the unique place. The place of Lot's wife is the right position to become a pillar of shame, and Bethel is the proper place to become a pillar for the building. When some Christians hear this, they will say, "Brother Lee, do you mean that only those in the church can become pillars of stone? What about those of us who are not in the church?" My answer is, "The surest way to become a pillar is to get into the church." We are all familiar with the need for insurance. You may be fortunate enough never to have an accident, but it is still wise to have insurance. When those outside the church argue with me about this matter, I have often said, "Friend, I have peace within me. Whether my way is right or wrong I really do not care. But I know that as long as I remain on this way, I am at peace. How about you? While you are arguing with me, do you have peace?" Many have said, "No, I don't have peace." Then I have replied, "Why do I have peace, yet you don't have it? It is because you are not on the way. Please don't argue with me." To all our Christian friends, I would say this word: "Come to Bethel and get into the church. This is the best insurance company. Here we are all insured." It is significant that, in chapters twenty-eight and thirty-five, Jacob set up a pillar in Bethel, in the house of God. Today, the house of God is the church. In 1 Timothy 3:15 Paul said, "But if I delay, that you may know how one ought to conduct himself in the house of God, which is the church of the living God, the pillar and base of the truth." If you would be a pillar of stone, you must be here in Bethel.

ee. Coming to Bethel Twice

Jacob came to Bethel twice. According to my experience, this indicates that we all come into the church twice. The first time we come in a dream, and the second time we come in actuality. In 1925, I had a clear dream, but it was not until seven years later, in 1932, that I came into the actuality and practicality of the church life. Many of you have had a similar experience. When you first came into the church, it was, for quite a period of time, a dream. You might have been in a dream for a number of years. But after those years, it was no longer a dream, and you could say, "Oh, I am actually and practically in the church life. The past years have been a dream. Thank the Lord for keeping me in this dream, but now I have the actual experience." Firstly, Jacob had the dream. More than twenty years later, he was brought into the experience.

If you compare chapters twenty-eight and thirty-five, you will see a great difference between them. Everything in chapter twenty-eight, being a dream, is somewhat vague; nothing is definite. In the experience in chapter thirty-five, however, everything is definite and practical. Nevertheless, we thank the Lord that the dream in the beginning was a true picture. Everything in the reality is the same as that in the dream.

In this, there is no difference. The only difference is that the dream is indefinite and that the actuality is definite. We need both the dream and the practicality. We praise the Lord that today we are in the practicality of the church life.

In the practicality of Bethel in chapter thirty-five, Jacob not only set up a pillar, but poured a drink offering upon it. In chapter twenty-eight there was no pouring out of a drink offering, only the pouring out of oil. But here, prior to the pouring out of the oil, there was the pouring out of the drink offering. This experience is very subjective. In Bethel, we firstly have the dream and then the actuality. In the actuality we build a pillar and pour ourselves upon it. This is very meaningful. Jacob did not pour out the drink offering upon himself or upon the earth; he poured it out upon the pillar. We shall see more of this in another message.

> ff. The Christ on Whom We Rest Being
> Constituted into a Pillar

According to 28:18, Jacob "took the stone that he had made his pillow, and set it up for a pillar" (Heb.). The pillar was the stone he had used for a pillow. This stone depicts Christ as our rest. Jacob did not have this dream when he was at home, but when he was traveling on his pilgrim journey. Like Jacob, we also are pilgrims. As we are traveling on our way, we see the vision of the church. Everyone who is on this pilgrim way is weary and needs rest. Where can we find this rest? The answer is the Lord's word in Matthew 11:28: "Come to Me all who labor and are burdened, and I will give you rest." Christ is the stone on which we may lay our weary head and find rest. The Christ on whom we rest is the constituent of the pillar. We ourselves are not the material for building the pillar. This material must be the Christ on whom we rest and whom we experience. It is the Christ wrought into our being who is constituted into the pillar.

In today's Christianity it is very difficult for people to have the constitution of the pillar because few have been instructed how to experience Christ in a subjective way. When you were in Christianity, were you ever told how to experience Christ's being wrought into you? Recently, I told some brothers and sisters that we in the church must not only love the Lord and live for Him—we must also live by Him. Oh, there is a vast difference between living for Christ and living by Christ. If you live for Christ, it is you who do things for Him, but you remain yourself and Christ is not wrought into your being. To live by Christ, however, means that Christ is wrought into us. By having Christ wrought into our being, we become material for the building. The stone for the pillar is firstly Christ. Following this, it is Christ experienced by us and wrought into us. Now this stone is not merely Christ, but Christ within us. Christ is wrought into our being, and we become one with Him. In this way, we become the building material for the pillar.

This experience is only possible in the church life. At the least, we can say that the greatest possibility of having this experience is in the church life. The reason for this is that outside the church, in the so-called Christian religion, very few are taught to have Christ wrought into them. I am fully assured that, from now on, message after message will be given instructing us how to live by Christ. This working of Christ into our being is true transformation. When the element of Christ is added into us, we become the material for the building of the pillar. This all takes place in Bethel, the place where Jacob was.

In 1964, I was invited to speak to a certain group in Dallas. My hosts, who appreciated my ministry, were very kind to me. However, they told me, both in plain words and by suggestions, that the people in Dallas were not ready to hear about the church. They said, "Brother Lee, please sympathize with us and do not say a word about the church." I did not promise to comply with their request. Rather, I said, "I fully realize the situation. But I assure you that the more I talk about Christ and minister Christ as life to the people, the more they will desire to have the church. Even if I do not say a word about the church and only minister Christ as life, they will still have the desire for the church." In the last meeting, I was burdened to speak a word about the church. When I stood up and asked the people to read Romans 12, they were disappointed. But I said to myself, "I don't care whether I offend you or not. If I do not release my burden, I cannot live." I then gave a strong word concerning the church, and they were offended by it. Later, I learned that a certain brother, who had not yet come into the church life, had attended that last meeting. Many had been praying for him. During that meeting, which was the only meeting he attended, he was caught for the church life. Although I had offended those people, the Lord gained this brother. Today, this brother has become a pillar.

gg. Being Perfected to Be a Pillar

How can you tell that someone has become a pillar? In the church life we realize that if certain brothers are taken away, everything collapses, but if they are present, they are pillars supporting the whole building. The Lord is not concerned about those who are offended; He cares for those who will become pillars. The pillars can only be perfected in Bethel. In other words, the pillars can only be set up in Bethel. No pillar for God's house has ever been set up outside of Bethel. If that brother whom I met in Dallas had not come into the church but had remained in a denomination, he could not have been perfected to be a pillar. He was perfected in Bethel, in the church life. After we experience Christ in a subjective way and are definitely and absolutely in the church life, we still need a great deal of perfection.

Let us consider further the pillars mentioned in Galatians 2:9. When the Lord called Peter, he was a fisherman. He was raw, wild, and unperfected. But after the Lord had spent three and a half years working on him, he was perfected and, on the day of Pentecost, he was set up as a pillar. When Peter stood up on the day of Pentecost, the angels might have rejoiced and said, "This is Boaz. This is the sign that God's building is coming." If you read the book of Acts, you will see that Peter was a pillar standing in front of the New Testament temple of God.

Young people, this is a word from my heart. The Lord's recovery is spreading, and I have the assurance that it will spread at a good pace. But the rate of the expansion of the Lord's recovery depends upon the pillars. I believe there will be churches in all the major cities of this country and in all the leading countries on earth. For this, there is the need of the pillars. I hope that you young people will see this. If you see it, you will say, "Lord, I cannot deny that You have appointed me to Your way and that I have heard Your up-to-date word. I realize that I must experience Christ in a subjective way and that I must be perfected in the church life in Bethel. Lord, have mercy on me and grant me the grace I need."

Young people, my burden is that you realize that your responsibility is tremendous. If during the coming years many of you will be perfected, the Lord's recovery will spread at a rapid speed. How much the Lord has done through those who have been perfected to be pillars! What do you think the Lord could do if He had a hundred more?

My burden is not simply to release a message. It is to help you see that today we all have the golden opportunity to be perfected and to be made pillars. Because we are at Bethel, our opportunity is much greater than Peter's was. Peter was in the Gospels, in the beginning of the New Testament, but we are at the end of the New Testament, even in Revelation 3:12. I believe that the opportunity we have today is unique in history. Never before has there been such a church life as there is today in Anaheim, and never before has the Lord's ministry of the Word been so bright and rich. Do not exercise your mentality or hold to your opinion. Your opinions will take you nowhere. Drop your opinions, love the Lord, take Him as your life and as your person, and live by Him in the church life. Learn of those who have become pillars. They have devoured, absorbed, and soaked in everything of the church and of this ministry. Follow them to know nothing and to daily be saturated with the church life and with the Word of God. If you do this, I believe that after a few years many of you will become pillars. Then wherever you go, the pillar, the signboard of God's building, will go with you. We all are in the church and under this ministry. Today is surely a golden opportunity ordained by the Lord.

LIFE-STUDY OF GENESIS

MESSAGE EIGHTY-THREE

BEING TRANSFORMED

(6)

I am still burdened about the pillar. Based upon the principle that nearly everything in the book of Genesis is a seed that is developed in the following books of the Bible, we come to 1 Kings 7:13-22, a strong portion in the Word regarding the pillars. In Jacob's calling, Jacob's being transformed was mainly related to this matter of the pillar. After his dream at Bethel, Jacob set up a pillar (28:18). When he returned to Bethel, he also set up a pillar (35:14). When Jacob set up the pillar the first time, he said, "This stone which I have set for a pillar, shall be God's house" (28:22). This indicates that the pillar was not only the pillar, but also that it would become Bethel, the house of God. In 1 Kings we have the first mention of the temple. Prior to that, there was the tabernacle, but no temple. The most striking feature of the exterior of the temple was the two pillars. In 1 Kings chapter seven we have a detailed picture of these pillars. I am burdened that, having considered the seed of the pillar in Genesis, we now look into the development of this seed in the following books of the Old Testament. Later, we shall consider the consummation of this seed in the New Testament.

(b) Related to the Building of the Temple

aa. By Solomon through Hiram

The pillars of the temple were built by Solomon through Hiram, "a worker in brass" who was "filled with wisdom, and understanding, and skill to work all works in brass" (1 Kings 7:14). Much of what is found in the Old Testament, such as the tabernacle and the temple, is a shadow, a type. We need to know the fulfillment of all these types. Solomon was a type of Christ, and Hiram was a type of the gifted person in the New Testament. Undoubtedly, the Apostle Paul was a gifted person; he was the New Testament Hiram. Ephesians 4:11 and 12 say, "And He gave some apostles, and some prophets, and some evangelists, and some shepherds and teachers, for the perfecting of the saints." The gifted persons are given by the Head to the Body to perfect the saints. That the pillars were not built by Solomon directly but by Solomon through Hiram indicates that today Christ does not build up the pillars directly but through the gifted persons. Thus, we must submit to the hands of the gifted persons, just as the brass was subject to the skilled and gifted hands of Hiram.

bb. Two Pillars

According to 1 Kings 7:15, Hiram "fashioned two pillars" (Heb.). In the Bible, the number two is the number of testimony. These two pillars stood in front of the temple as a testimony. The thought concerning the pillar in the book of Genesis is that of testimony. After Jacob had arranged a settlement with Laban, he "took a stone, and set it up for a pillar" (31:45), and this pillar was a testimony (31:51-52). Undoubtedly, when Jacob set up the pillar in chapter twenty-eight, his concept was also that of a testimony. Under the inspiration of the Spirit of God, he said that this testimony would be the house of God. The temple in the Old Testament certainly was a testimony to God. The principle is the same with respect to the church today. According to 1 Timothy 3:15, the house of God, which is the church, is the pillar. This means that the church as a whole stands on earth to testify God to the universe. Therefore, the two pillars in front of the temple in the Old Testament were a strong testimony of God's building.

cc. Of Brass

Now we come to a crucial point—the two pillars were made of brass (1 Kings 7:15). In Genesis the pillar is a pillar of stone, but in 1 Kings 7 the pillars are pillars of brass. A stone indicates transformation. Although we are clay, we can be transformed into stone. But what does brass signify? It signifies God's judgment. For example, the altar at the entrance of the tabernacle was covered with brass indicating God's judgment (Exo. 27:1-2; Num. 16:38-40). The laver was also made of brass (Exo. 30:18). Furthermore, the serpent of brass put on a pole (Num. 21:8-9) also testified of Christ's being judged by God on our behalf (John 3:14). Therefore, in typology, brass always signifies God's judgment. That the two pillars were made of brass clearly indicates that if we would be a pillar, we must realize that we are those under God's judgment. We should not only be under God's judgment, but also under our own judgment. Like Paul in Galatians 2:20, we must say, "I have been crucified. I have been crucified because I am not good for anything in God's economy. I am only qualified for death." Many brothers are intelligent and capable and many sisters are quite nice. Nevertheless, we must recognize that actually we are not good at all. We are not even worth a penny. We are only good for death. To say, "I have been put aside, condemned, and put to death," is a type of self-judgment. What is your judgment regarding yourself? You must answer, "My judgment of myself is that I am good for nothing and that I have been crucified."

If you think that you are qualified to be a pillar, then you are already disqualified. Let me relate something concerning Brother Nee's practice relating to the appointment of elders. Brother Nee said that no one who was ambitious to be an elder should ever be an elder. Therefore, many of us in mainland China said, "Don't think that you can be an elder and do not be ambitious to be an elder. If you are ambitious to be an elder, you can never be one." When I first came to Shanghai in 1933, I met a certain brother. I later discovered that he was very ambitious to be an elder. Brother Nee told me that just because this brother was so ambitious to be an elder he was not qualified to be an elder. Whoever is ambitious to be an elder is disqualified from being one. More or less, as some brothers can testify, we have practiced this during these years in the United States. A few among us have hunted for eldership. They have even moved from place to place seeking an opportunity to be an elder. After realizing that the eldership in a particular locality had been filled up, they moved to another locality where there were many openings. However, those openings could only be filled by those who had no ambition to be elders. Once we discover that a brother is ambitious to be an elder, he will be fully disqualified for eternity. The reason for this is that such a brother is not a person under God's judgment. We all must say, "I am not qualified. I am poor, sinful, fallen, and corrupt." Moreover, we must say, "Lord, I am so fallen, sinful, and corrupt. How could I bear the responsibility of the eldership? I am not qualified for this." This is the experience of brass. To justify ourselves and to qualify ourselves is to be through with the brass. Those who experience brass are those who are constantly under judgment.

During the early years in China, I sometimes wondered why Brother Nee was so strict in this matter. Eventually, I learned that whoever was ambitious to be a leader in any aspect of the church life became a problem. There was not one exception to this. However, all those who became a true profit to the building of the church were those who did not think of themselves as being qualified for leadership. Rather, they always said, "I am not qualified. I am too poor. My disposition is not suitable, and I am still too much in my natural life. I do not consider myself to be good." To say this is not only to be under God's judgment, but also under self-judgment. What is your evaluation of yourself? Do not say, "No one else is good except me." Whenever you say this, you are finished, and the Lord would never put His seal upon this evaluation of yourself. We all must have the realization that we are fallen, corrupt, and no good. We all must feel that in us, that is, in our flesh, there is nothing good (Rom. 7:18). We should say, "I am worthy of nothing but death. How could the brothers think that I should be one of the elders? I am terrified of this possibility." I do not speak this in vain. In the past years some have said, "Why was Brother So-and-so appointed to be an elder and I was not?" He was appointed instead of you because you feel that you are qualified. Your self-approval disqualifies you. The Lord will never choose anyone who considers himself to be qualified. If you think that you are qualified, then you have nothing to do with brass. Instead, you are self-made gold. The experience of brass is that we are always under God's judgment and under our own self-judgment. We all must apply this word to ourselves, saying, "Lord, have mercy upon me, for in me there is nothing good." This is the reason that we have been crucified. If we think there is something good in us, we are liars.

In Galatians 2:20 Paul said, "It is no longer I who live, but Christ lives in me." We may also apply his word in 1 Corinthians 15:10, which says, "But by the grace of God I am what I am; and His grace unto me was not in vain, but I labored more abundantly than all of them, yet not I, but the grace of God with me." In Galatians 2:20, Paul said, "No longer I who live, but Christ" and in 1 Corinthians 15:10, he said, "Not I, but the grace of God." Paul seemed to be saying, "Whatever I am, I am by the grace of God. By myself, I am nothing. By myself, I could never be an apostle or a minister of God's living word. I labored more than the others, but it was not I who labored—it was the grace of God." This is the experience of brass.

In typology and in figure, the two brass pillars in 1 Kings 7 tell us that we must be under God's judgment as well as under our own self-judgment. We must judge ourselves as being nothing and as being only qualified to be crucified. I say this not only to the brothers, but also to the sisters. None of us is good for anything. We must consider ourselves as those under God's judgment. If an elder is not under God's judgment, he cannot be a good elder, and if a leading sister is not under God's judgment, she cannot be a proper leading sister. I fully realize and can testify that in order to minister the Word of God, I must always be under self-judgment. While I may spend only a short time praying positively for the meeting, I may spend a long time in self-judgment, judging myself as being poor, unworthy, fleshly, and natural. Sometimes, I even sigh and groan, saying, "O Lord, when will the time come that I can minister Your word apart from my flesh?" Do not think that as I stand here ministering to you, I am so good. No, I am too poor. As long as we are in the natural life and in the old creation, we are pitiful. We must serve under God's judgment and minister under our own realization of God's judgment. I am one who has already been judged. My natural being, my flesh, and my self have all been judged by God, and I am still under this judgment. If we have this realization, then we become brass.

Although the brass shines, it has no glory. With the shining of gold, on the contrary, there is glory. The shining of brass signifies that we are under God's judgment. If an elder shines like brass, then he is an elder who has been and who still is under God's judgment. He is not the golden lampstand standing for God's glory; he is the brass pillar standing for God's judgment. Do you intend to be a pillar or a leader among the children of God? If you do, then you must be under God's judgment. I hope that the Holy Spirit will speak this to you. In the temple of God there is no pride, no self-boasting. In the temple of God, the pillars are of brass. Those who bear the burden are judged beings. All the elders are brothers who have been and who are still under God's judgment. Furthermore, this judgment is fully realized by themselves. They recognize that they are under God's judgment because they are sinful, fallen, and corrupted, because there is nothing good in them, and because they are not qualified for anything in God's economy. I could repeat this word again and again and again. Do you know why there is so much fighting in Christianity? It is because there is no brass. There is no judgment by God. Rather, all the "pillars" there are wooden columns. The more responsibility you bear in the proper church life, the more you must realize that you are under God's judgment. You are just brass under the judgment of God. Do not release yourself from this judgment even for a moment. Instead, you must remain under the realization of God's judgment and stay with the brass.

dd. Eighteen Cubits High Apiece

The pillars were "eighteen cubits high apiece" (1 Kings 7:15). As we shall see, the circumference of each pillar was twelve cubits. Eighteen cubits is half of three units of twelve cubits. In other words, eighteen is half of three complete units. The three units signify the very Triune God who has been dispensed into us. If we would be pillars, we must firstly judge ourselves and then be filled, saturated, and permeated with the Triune God. As I was wondering why each pillar was a half of three complete units, the Lord said, "Stupid man, have you not given several messages saying that the standing boards in the tabernacle were each one and a half cubits wide? Didn't you say that no board could stand by itself, but that it had to stand with another? Don't you see that it is the same with the pillars? Just as the two boards standing together made three complete cubits, so the two pillars make three complete units." Then I said, "Now I understand, Lord."

If you would be a pillar, you must be filled, saturated, and permeated with the Triune God. However, no matter how much you have been filled with God, you are still only a part. At most, you are one half. You can never have God completely. The very God who is in you is also in your brother. Because you are not a full unit, you need others to complete you. All the spiritual giants think that they can be complete individualistically. But the Bible reveals that everyone is only a half. The standing boards in the tabernacle were a half (Exo. 26:15-16), and each of the pillars in the temple is a half.

When they hear this, some may say, "Brother Lee is allegorizing the Bible." If I am allegorizing, then I have the ground to allegorize. Why does the Bible not say that the pillars were seventeen or nineteen cubits high? Would it be possible to allegorize if the pillars were this height? No, it would be impossible. But, as I was seeking the Lord, He showed me that in this section of the Word twelve is the complete unit and eighteen is one and a half units. This indicates that although we might be filled with the Triune God, God will never wholly commit Himself to us individually. No matter how much of God we gain, we are not the whole; we are only a part. We need one another. I need you, and you need me. The Lord always sent out His disciples two by two (Mark 6:7; Luke 10:1; Acts 13:2). I am not the number thirty-six. At most, I am the number eighteen. No matter how tall you are, you must realize that you are only eighteen cubits and that you need others. Do not say, "I am perfect and complete. You all need me, but I don't need you." It is foolish to say this. At most, we can be only eighteen cubits. Some sisters dream about being filled with God. But no matter how much they are filled with Him, they could never be more than half a unit. They need others.

ee. Twelve Cubits Round

Now we come to the circumference of the pillars. First Kings 7:15 says, "A line of twelve cubits did compass either of them about." As far as language is concerned, the composition of this verse is very peculiar. Instead of speaking of the circumference, it says that a "line of twelve cubits" encompassed the pillars. Even this rendering is not an exact, literal translation; it is somewhat of an interpretation. One version says, "a circumference of twelve cubits." This rendering is simple and I prefer it. Nevertheless, the Bible has no waste of words, and we must consider the meaning of the actual composition of this verse. It means to use a thread as a line to measure around the pillars. The purpose of this is to impress us with the completion and perfection of our being mingled with God in His eternal administration. The number seven, which signifies perfection and completion in God's move in this age, is composed of four plus three. This is a matter of addition. But the number twelve, which is composed of four times three, is a matter of multiplication, indicating that the creature is mingled with the Triune God and that this mingling must be complete and perfect in God's eternal administration. The pillars are not square, rectangular, or triangular; they are round, circular, signifying that their perfection is eternal.

As we put together the brass, the height of eighteen cubits, and the circumference of twelve cubits, we see that in order to be a pillar we must be under God's judgment and that we must be fully, thoroughly, and completely saturated with God. We must be brass and we must be twelve cubits around. Nevertheless, no matter how completely we have been mingled with God, we are still only a half; we need another half. If any elder is like this, he will certainly be an outstanding elder. If any leading sister is like this, she will be a most excellent sister. This kind of person certainly can bear the responsibility.

Our problem is that we do not condemn ourselves. Rather, we vindicate, justify, approve, and excuse ourselves. Often we say, "That is not my mistake; it is Brother So-and-so's mistake. I am always careful. I am not wrong." This is self-vindication. After we vindicate ourselves, we proceed to justify and approve ourselves. We do not need to be tested, for we have already approved ourselves. In our eyes, there is no problem with ourselves. Sometimes, however, we are caught in a mistake. Then we excuse ourselves, perhaps by saying, "I made that mistake because the meeting was so long and I was tired." How often we make exits for ourselves! We have four big exits: self-vindication, self-justification, self-approval, and self-excuse. Even when we are caught in a mistake, we still excuse ourselves. For example, a sister may say, "I type poorly because the others have the best typewriters and the worst typewriter is allotted to me." In the past, I have had a lot of self-vindication, self-justification, self-approval, and self-excuse.

Very rarely does a husband or wife at the beginning of an argument, say, "I'm sorry. This is my mistake. Please forgive me." Rather, the wife says, "Do you know why I was so strong with my husband? It was because he is always late. Throughout our whole marriage, his lateness has troubled me." Then the husband will say, "My wife never sympathizes with me. I am busy and have a great deal of work to do. When I am overworked like this, how can I help being late?" This is self-vindication, self-justification, self-approval, and self-excuse. If we would daily crucify these four things, there would be no fighting whatever in our homes.

It is inadequate for us simply to be the number four. We must be number seven—four plus the Triune God. This, however, is still the initial stage, not the consummation, which is the number twelve. In order to be the number twelve, we must be filled, saturated, and mingled with God. When we are fully saturated and mingled with God, we are adequate for God's eternal administration. Nevertheless, as we have pointed out, even after we have become the number twelve, we are still only eighteen cubits in height. We are only half a unit. If we were all like this, there would be no problems. Instead of fighting with others, we would condemn ourselves, saying, "Lord, I need You. I have been crucified, and Christ lives in me. It is not I, but the grace of God that is with me." This is the brass, the judgment, and the twelve cubits, the mingling of God with man. Since we are, at most, only a half, we need others for God's economy and administration. If you pray over these points, you will see that this is the pillar that can bear the responsibility in the house of God.

ff. Two Capitals

On the top of each of the pillars was a capital five cubits in height (1 Kings 7:16). The capitals were the top coverings of the pillars. The fact that each capital was five cubits in height and not six or seven cubits is significant. As we have pointed out several times, in the Bible the number five denotes responsibility. Consider your hand: the four fingers and the thumb are for bearing responsibility. If we had just four fingers, we could not bear responsibility in a proper way. The number four signifies the creature, and the number one signifies the unique God. When the unique God is added to human beings, our number becomes five.

For example, the ten commandments were written in groups of five on two tables of stone, and the ten virgins were divided into five wise ones and five foolish ones. Therefore, the two capitals five cubits in height indicate the bearing of responsibility. If you say that this is my allegorization, I would reply that I have the ground to allegorize, for we are not told that the capitals are four and a half or six cubits in height, but that they are five cubits in height. The combined height of the two capitals totals ten cubits. The number ten signifies fullness in responsibility. Both the ten commandments and the ten virgins indicate fullness. Therefore, in the Bible the number ten reveals fullness of human responsibility toward God. Our ten fingers for working and ten toes for moving and walking indicate this.

gg. Nets of Checkerwork and Wreaths of Chainwork

First Kings 7:17 speaks of "nets of checkerwork, and wreaths of chainwork, for the capitals which were upon the top of the pillars; seven for the one capital, and seven for the other capital" (Heb.). To what do the nets of checkerwork and wreaths of chainwork refer? After consulting many versions, I discovered that the checkerwork resembles a trellis, a frame with small square holes that bears a vine. Furthermore, the word "work" in this verse implies a design. Hence, checkerwork is a checker design and chainwork a chain design. As we shall see, this checker design is for the growth of the lilies. This trellis is the setting for the lilies. In a sense, it is a net to hold the lilies. The chainwork is like a wreath encompassing the outside of the capital. Hence, upon the capitals are nets of checkerwork and wreaths of chainwork.

What does all this signify? We have seen that the number five, the height of the capitals, denotes responsibility, and that two times five means fullness of responsibility. But why are there also on these capitals nets of checkerwork and wreaths of chainwork? While I was burdened to understand this, the Lord showed me that this is the intermixed and complicated situation. The burden and responsibility borne by the pillars in the family, in the church, and in the ministry is always in a complicated and intermixed situation. We may often like to straighten out these situations, but we cannot do it. If you straighten out one complication, there will be three others to take its place. If you attempt to make one matter clear, the situation will become even more unclear. The more you try to make it understandable, the more it will be misunderstood. Do not say, "Last night Brother So-and-so was unhappy with his wife." If you talk like this, you will be involved. The more we try to explain ourselves, the more misunderstanding there will be, and this misunderstanding will multiply. Through many years of experience, I have learned that the best way to avoid misunderstanding is to say as little as possible. Sometimes, you should not even say the words, "Praise the Lord," to your wife. If you do this, she may say, "Why are you so spiritual? Don't you realize that your praising condemns me? When you praise the Lord, you are saying that you are spiritual and that I am carnal." The church life is a checkerwork surrounded by a chain, and the eldership is a most intricate trellis with the strongest chain.

I know of a certain dear one who holds the concept that wherever he is, those around him should be like angels. They should all be very spiritual, going to bed early and rising early in the morning to pray-read the Word. If everyone would be heavenly, then this dear one would be happy. But there is no place on earth like the one envisioned by this dear one. In many homes, some stay up late talking and then sleep until late in the morning. Upon waking, some may complain that it was too cold with the window open all night, and others may complain that it was so stuffy that they felt like they were suffocating.

Every situation faced by the church members is a checkerwork, a trellis encircled by a crown of pins and thorns. I have a large family and I am also in a large church. I have many children and grandchildren and many dear brothers and sisters. Wherever I am, in Taipei or in Anaheim, I cannot escape the checkerwork and chainwork. In a sense, Anaheim is wonderful, but it is full of checkerwork and chains. Even the angels know that I am constantly in an intermixed and complicated situation. My children and all the problems brought to me by the brothers and sisters in the churches create more checkerwork for me. It is our destiny to be in this situation. We must not only bear the responsibility in this intermixed and complicated situation, but also live in the midst of it.

hh. The Capitals Being of Lily Work

In order to bear the responsibility in this complicated situation, we must live by faith in God. First Kings 7:19 says, "And the capitals that were upon the top of the pillars in the porch were of lily work" (Heb.). The lily signifies a life of faith in God. Firstly, we must condemn ourselves, realizing that we are fallen, incapable, unqualified, and that we are nothing. Then we must live by faith in God, not by what we are or by what we can do. We must be a lily existing by what God is to us, not by what we are (Matt. 6:28, 30). Our living on earth today depends upon Him. How can we possibly bear the responsibility in the intermixed and complicated church life? In ourselves, we are incapable of doing this, but we can do so if we live by faith in God. It is not I, but Christ who lives in me—this is the lily. It is not I who bear the responsibility—it is He who bears it. I live, not by myself, but by Him, and I minister, not by myself, but by Him. If you sisters are mothers in the church life, you must say, "I am not a mother in the church by myself, but by Him." In Song of Songs 2:1 and 2 the seeker says, "I am the lily of the valley." Then the Lord replies, "As the lily among thorns, so is my love among the daughters."

What earthly architect would have designed a brass pillar bearing brass capitals with lily work on the top of them? Humanly speaking, this is not meaningful, but spiritually speaking, it is very significant. On the one hand, we are the condemned and judged brass; on the other hand, we are the living lilies. The brass means, "Not I," and the lily means, "But Christ." Those who are lilies can say, "The life that I now live, I live by the faith of Jesus Christ." By all this we can realize that we are lilies bearing an impossible responsibility in an intermixed and complicated situation full of checkerwork and chainwork. The elders should not say, "Lord, take these complications away." Rather, they should expect more complications. I am quite certain that the more you pray for the complications to be reduced, the more complications there will be. All the checkerwork is the base, the bed, in which the lilies grow.

According to the context, the chainwork, being wreaths, was a form of decoration. But this decoration is filled with complications. When you come to my home, do not expect everything there to be clear and simple. If you stay with me for a while, you will find many complications and complaints. But all this is the beauty of my family, for it is a wreath, a crown. Every elder expects the church life to be clear-cut like a Chinese bean cake where every piece is cut square and neat. They want everything in the church to be accurate and fine. The only place like this is the cemetery. The proper church life, like the church life in Anaheim, is a net of checkerwork and a wreath of chainwork. This is the place where the elders bear the responsibility in full. This cannot be understood simply by studying the passage, but by interpreting this portion of the Word in the light of our experience.

ii. Two Hundred Pomegranates

Verse 20 says, "And the capitals upon the two pillars had pomegranates also above, over against the belly which was by the network: and the pomegranates were two hundred in rows round about upon the other capital" (Heb.). Hallelujah for the two hundred pomegranates! Around each capital was a projection, like a belly. Encompassing the projection on each capital were two rows of a hundred pomegranates each. This indicates two times of a hundredfold expression of the riches of life. If you contact these elders who daily bear the responsibility in the intermixed and complicated situation, you will see that they express pomegranates, the riches of life. All the complaints, dissatisfactions, and troubling telephone calls eventually form a projection full of pomegranates. How wonderful this is!

jj. The Capitals Being Four Cubits in Diameter

The diameter of each of the capitals is four cubits (1 Kings 7:19). This indicates that the number twelve, the circumference of the pillars, is composed of four times three. While the circumference of the pillar is twelve cubits, the diameter of the capitals is four cubits. This implies that the pillars with their capitals are the number four, that is, the creatures, human beings, but that they are multiplied by the Triune God. Being mingled with the Triune God, they eventually become the number twelve. If you put all this together, you will see that it is very meaningful. It implies that those who judge and condemn themselves and count themselves as nothing will be able to bear the responsibility in full in the midst of a complicated situation because they do not live by themselves but by God. Eventually, they do not express their capability, qualification, intelligence, understanding, and wisdom—they express pomegranates, the riches of life two-hundredfold.

kk. Two Pillars Standing in the Porch of the Temple

Finally, we are told that the names of these two pillars were Jachin and Boaz (1 Kings 7:21). Jachin means, "He shall establish," and Boaz means, "In it is strength." These two pillars standing on the porch testify that the Lord will establish His building and that genuine strength is in the building. Even today, the building of the church gives this testimony. By the details of the picture in 1 Kings 7, we see how we can be a pillar in the building of God, judging ourselves, living by faith, bearing the responsibility, and expressing the riches of life.

LIFE-STUDY OF GENESIS

MESSAGE EIGHTY-FOUR

BEING TRANSFORMED

(7)

In this message we shall again devote our attention to the two pillars at the temple. We have seen that when Jacob was first at Bethel, he set up as a pillar the stone he had used for a pillow and called it the house of God (28:18, 22). We have pointed out again and again that nearly everything in the book of Genesis is a seed that is developed in the following books of the Bible. The full development of the seed of the pillar is in Revelation 3:12, where the Lord Jesus says, "He who overcomes, I will make him a pillar in the temple of My God." Between Genesis and Revelation, there are many portions of the Word concerning the pillars. Each time the two pillars at the temple are mentioned we see more of the details regarding them. Not every aspect of the pillars is found in any single portion.

Today's Christians have very little concern for God's building, which is for the accomplishment of God's economy. Although most Christians neglect this, the Bible strongly emphasizes it. If we would know the building, according to the biblical way, we must firstly see the pillar, for the pillar is a signboard of God's building. If we see what the pillar is and decide to become a pillar, then we are on the way of God's building. The pillar is so crucial that the Bible mentions it over and over again. Because most Christians have no understanding of God's building, they do not pay attention to those portions of Scripture which mention the pillar. But by the Lord's mercy we have been so deeply impressed with the pillar that we simply cannot get away from it. The Bible has no wasted words. Hence, whatever it reveals is meaningful and crucial for us. Because, at this end time, God is completing

His building, we must carefully consider what the pillar is and how we can become a pillar.

I would like now to stress three positive aspects and two negative aspects of the pillars covered in the last message. The three positive aspects are the brass, the lily, and the pomegranates. The pillars themselves were made of brass. On the top of the capital were the lilies and around the capital were the pomegranates. I doubt that any human designer would ever have put these three things together. But how crucial and meaningful it all is to us! Brass signifies death under judgment. We must be under judgment, realizing that we are good for nothing but death and that we have been crucified (Gal. 2:20). Furthermore, we all have been buried in baptism (Rom. 6:4). Thus, we are a people under the judgment of death. But after death comes resurrection, and the lily grows upon us in resurrection. The pomegranates surrounding the capital signify the expression of the riches of life. Therefore, in the pillars we see death, resurrection, and the expression of life. Praise the Lord that many of us can testify that day by day we are the brass growing lilies and expressing pomegranates. Are you not such a person? If you are not, then you are not qualified to be a pillar and you have nothing to do with God's building.

The two negative aspects of the pillars are the checkerwork (the network) and the chainwork. The checkerwork and chainwork signify the intermixed and complicated situation. The checkerwork is a lattice composed of intersecting bars. This indicates that, in our experience, we are daily being crossed out. As we undergo this, we are held by the chainwork. Many times we brothers are under the crossing out of our dear wives. Although we may desire to escape this, we are held by the chains and cannot slip away. We may be cut into pieces, but not one piece can escape. The sisters can all testify of the same thing in relation to their husbands. Some in the church life say that they cannot bear the crossing out of the elders. However, the chainwork is also there. In the church life we have both the checkerwork and the chainwork. Praise the Lord for these two negative things, because the brass, the lily, and the pomegranates can only be connected by them.

Not long after I was saved, I learned that I had been crucified with Christ. But I did not know how this crucifixion could practically be applied to me. It is applied by the checkerwork, the network. Without the network and the chainwork, our co-crucifixion with Christ and His living instead of us would be mere doctrine. We may know the doctrine of being crucified with Christ and recite Galatians 2:20 over and over only to discover that this does not avail. I did this again and again without success. I repeated the words, "I have been crucified with Christ, and it is no longer I who live, but Christ lives in me." Later, I experienced the network and the chainwork in the church life. It has been through these two negative things that the crucifixion and resurrection of Christ have been practically applied to my life. Eventually, therefore, the three positive things and the two negative things become one unit. We have the brass, the lily, and the pomegranates joined by the checkerwork and the chainwork. All five are joined in the pillar.

11. Two Bowls of the Two Capitals on the Top of the Two Pillars, Two Cubits High

In addition to all the points covered in the previous message, we must cover nine further points in this message. God, His Word, and His dealing with us are not simple.

On the top of the capitals which were on the pillars were two bowls (2 Chron. 4:12; 2 Kings 25:17). Each bowl, including the network, was two cubits high (see definition below). What does this signify? The bowls are round. (Darby translates the Hebrew word for bowls as "globes.") On the top of each capital there were two bowls, one above the other. Around the capitals were "chains like a necklace," or "chains at the collar," (2 Chron. 3:16, Amplified Bible; Darby's New Translation) that divided the capital into two sections. The first section was the base. Although 1 Kings 7:16 says that the capitals were five cubits high, 2 Kings 25:17 says that the capitals were three cubits high. The reason for this is that three cubits is the height of the base of the capital and five cubits is the height of the whole capital. In other words, there were three cubits for the base and two for the bowls. Here, the number three does not signify the Triune God. Rather, it signifies the process of resurrection. In the Bible, two numbers, three and eight, signify resurrection. Three signifies the process of resurrection, and eight, the first day of a new week, denotes the freshness of resurrection, the new beginning in resurrection. The three cubits of the base of the capital are closely related to the network and the chainwork. This reveals that the network and the chainwork are for the process of resurrection. Moreover, the number two, the height of the two bowls, signifies testimony. The two cubits of the two bowls on the two capitals of the two pillars signify testimony by living as a lily and by expressing the riches of life.

If you read all the portions concerning the two pillars, you will realize that the bowls are composed of the network, the chainwork, the lilies, and the pomegranates. The pomegranates are not on the base of the capital, but on the chainwork surrounding the bowls. The network covers the bowls, the chainwork surrounds the bowls, the pomegranates are upon the chainwork, and the lily grows upon the network. All these things together are the bowl. If you consider this in the light of your experience, you will realize that through the crossing out by the network and the restriction of the chainwork, you live as a lily to express the riches of the life of Christ. This is a living testimony coming out of the process of resurrection.

In our homes we are in the checkerwork and held by the chainwork. This is also true with the brothers and sisters in the church. Those who serve in the business office have undoubtedly experienced the checkerwork and the chainwork there. Surely in the business office there is much checkerwork and chainwork. But along with the checkerwork and the chainwork, there are also the three days. All those who serve in the business office are on the way of the three days, that is, they are in the process of resurrection.

The lilies appear on the top of the bowls on the third day. It does not matter how nice, gentle, or humble we are, for none of this is the lily. Rather, it is our natural life. The more we experience the crossing out, the more the lily grows on the third day. Every brother desires to have a nice wife, and every sister wants a gentle husband. However, no matter how nice or gentle we are, we are not lilies. The lily only grows on the third day in the midst of the checkerwork and the chainwork. When in all the intermixed and complicated situations we come to the third day, the lily will grow. Then we shall also have the pomegranates, the expression of the riches of life. This is the bowl—the glory, beauty, decoration, and crown. This is a testimony. I hope that the Spirit will speak more of this to you.

We all have been judged and we need to judge ourselves under God's judgment. It is easy to be a brass pillar, saying, "I'm fallen, corrupted, sinful, and good for nothing but death." But to pass through the three days of the process of resurrection in the midst of the crossing out of the checkerwork and the limitation of the chainwork is very difficult. But the more we are in the checkerwork and the chainwork, the more we are in the three days, the more the lily grows, and the more of the pomegranates we express. Then we become a living testimony, not of anything natural, but of the process of resurrection under the crossing out of the checkerwork and the restraint of the chainwork. There is no escape. We must stay in the checkerwork and chainwork. It is exactly like being buried for three days and coming out through the process of resurrection. As we pass through this experience, the lily grows and the pomegranates are expressed. Every pillar must bear the testimony of living by faith to express the riches of Christ through the process of resurrection under the crossing out of the checkerwork and the restriction of the chainwork. The brass in the two pillars in front of the temple indicates that we are under the death-judgment, which brings us into the process of resurrection, signified by the three-cubit height of the base of the capitals. This process of resurrection brings us through the network and the chainwork to grow the lily and to bear the pomegranates for a testimony. This is the way for the pillar to bear the responsibility, signified by the five cubits, the total height of the capitals.

The bowls on the capitals were not square, but round. This roundness signifies that living by faith in God and bearing responsibility in the midst of all the complications is not legal but always flexible. When we live in the Spirit, nothing is legal. Rather, we are flexible in every situation. Both the young and the old are legal. The old have their old legal way, and the young have their fresh legal way. Because of this, I am reluctant to give many instructions during the training. If I do this, all the young will take these instructions in a fresh legal way. Nearly every Christian is legally square. If we are not square, then we are triangular or even pentagonal. Some of the older sisters like to eat and go to bed at an exact time. This legality has killed many of the young people. While it is good for you to be regulated, for the sake of others, you need to be flexible. Some elders are very square. However, others are so round that they are political. A politician has no sides. Although we should be round we should not be politically round. Those who serve in the business office should be round. If you are square in your serving, you will kill everyone. Instead of being square, you must be flexible to fit into every situation. This is the way we should be in our daily living. As we are in the midst of the checkerwork and the chainwork, we must be flexible.

mm. Four Hundred Pomegranates on the Two Networks

Second Chronicles 4:13 says that there were "four hundred pomegranates on the two networks, two rows of pomegranates on each network, to cover the two bowls of the capitals which were upon the pillars" (Heb.). There were four hundred pomegranates on the two networks, with two rows on each network to cover the two bowls of the capitals upon the pillars. Why does it not say that there were three hundred or five hundred pomegranates? The Lord Jesus said that we can bear fruit thirtyfold, sixtyfold, and a hundredfold (Matt. 13:8). The hundredfold increase is the highest. Thus, we can express the riches of life a hundredfold. We know that the number four signifies us, the human creatures. The hundredfold expression of the riches of life is upon the creatures. That the four hundred pomegranates were arranged in two rows on each of the two pillars indicates a testimony. We must be strong, not simply in declaring that we are the testimony of Jesus, but in having a testimony by living. We need a testimony of the experience of the riches of the life of Christ four hundredfold. Although we may have problems in the church life, in our work, and at home, we also have the life of the lily, which, in the Bible, signifies a life lived by trusting in God. The Lord knows that I daily have one problem after another. If we live by ourselves, we cannot bear these problems. But we are lilies among thorns (S. S. 2:2). The thorns are just the problems. Our wife, children, grandchildren, the elders, and the co-workers are all "thorns." Although I am surrounded by so many "thorns," I praise the Lord that I am still living. I have not been "thorned" to death. I am living today, not like a giant, but like a lily. I do not live by my ability, but by faith in my God. I am simply a lily among thorns. The more thorns there are, the better, because the thorns give the opportunity for the Lord's ability to be expressed. We are different from the worldly people, who have no God in whom to trust.

Many seeking Christians are looking for a church life that is heavenly in every respect. They want everyone in this heavenly church life to be an angel. I am not imagining this; I have actually met people like this. Many of these seeking ones have traveled from "church" to "church" in pursuit of such a heavenly "church." If they find one, their heavenly "church" is soon exposed to be more than earthly. The way to determine whether or not a church is proper is mainly by the ground of the church, not by our measure of the heavenliness of the church. Today on earth there is not an angelic, heavenly church. Shortly after coming into the church life, you will find yourself in the midst of "thorns" and you will say, "I thought everyone here was an angel. But now I see that many of them are not angels but thorns. I cannot bear this." Although I may be a "thorn" to you, you also are a "thorn" to me. Eventually, we "thorn" one another and love one another. This "thorning" helps us grow. During the past three years in Anaheim, this "thorning" has helped us to grow. If everything in the church were smooth and angelic, there would be no testimony of the riches of life.

nn. Out of One Hundred Pomegranates, Ninety-six Being Exposed to the Open Air

Out of one hundred pomegranates, ninety-six were exposed to the open air (Jer. 52:23). Since every row had one hundred pomegranates, why did Jeremiah 52:23 suddenly speak of ninety-six pomegranates? Because the record in Jeremiah 52:23 concerns the destruction of the pillars by the Babylonian army, some think that four of the pomegranates on each row of chainwork were broken. But if you read this chapter carefully, you will see that this was not the case. The King James Version says, "There were ninety and six pomegranates on a side." This rendering is incorrect. The Hebrew words translated "on a side" should be "towards the air." Hence, this verse should read, "There were ninety and six pomegranates towards the air, and all the pomegranates upon the network were an hundred round about." Notice that all the pomegranates upon the network numbered one hundred. All were there, but only ninety-six were towards the air. The Hebrew word translated "side" in the King James Version is *ruach*, the word for spirit, wind, breath, and air. *Ruach* denotes something real yet invisible. The New American Standard Version says that there were ninety-six "exposed pomegranates." However, the margin gives the literal translation of "windward," which means towards the wind or towards the air.

Ninety-six pomegranates were exposed and four were covered. What is the significance of this? Ninety-six is composed of twelve times eight. Twelve signifies eternal completion, eight signifies resurrection, and the air signifies the Spirit. Therefore, the expression of the riches of life is eternally complete, in resurrection, and in the Spirit. This is the nature and atmosphere of our expression of life. Our expression of the riches of life is twelve, eternal; it is not seven, temporal. Moreover, it is also the number eight, the freshness of resurrection, not the number three, the process of resurrection. Here, it is not the process of resurrection, but the freshness, the beginning, the new start, of resurrection. Also, it is absolutely a matter in the Spirit. That the ninety-six pomegranates were exposed to the open air means that the expression of the riches of life is in the reality of the spiritual air, which is invisible. While we can sense it, we cannot touch it. In John 3:8, the Lord Jesus spoke of both the wind and the Spirit, saying, "The wind blows where it wills, and you hear the sound of it, but you do not know where it comes from and where it is going; so is everyone who is born of the Spirit." The regeneration of the Spirit resembles the moving of the wind. The wind blows and the Spirit regenerates. Our expression of the riches of life is not only eternal and in the freshness of resurrection, but is absolutely in the atmosphere of the Spirit. Whenever people see upon us the expression of the riches of life, they will immediately sense that they are in the Spirit and that there is some fresh wind, air, and atmosphere there. However, whenever we enter into a situation filled with death, we sense stuffiness. But when we are in a situation filled with the expression of the riches of life, we find ourselves in a spiritual atmosphere and sense that refreshing air is present. This is what it means for ninety-six pomegranates to be towards the air.

oo. Of the Four Hundred Pomegranates, Sixteen (Four of Each Hundred) Being Hidden

Of each hundred pomegranates, four were hidden. Because the Bible has no wasted words, there must be some significance relating to our experience in this verse. The only way I can understand it is by experience. That four of every one hundred pomegranates were hidden indicates that while our expression of the riches of life is eternal, in resurrection, and in the Spirit, our natural being, signified by the number four, must be covered. Our natural life, our natural being, our self, and our ego must be wholly concealed. Although I have sought to discover how these pomegranates were hidden, I have been unable to do so. It is a mystery known only to the Lord. However, if we examine our experience, we shall say, "Amen." When the riches of Christ are expressed, others can see the eternal expression of the riches of life in resurrection and in the atmosphere of the Spirit, but it is difficult to say where our natural man is. How meaningful it is to see that our ego is covered! Whenever "I" appears, the big number four will be there, but the ninety-six will be gone. Instead of air, there will just be the natural life, the old man, and the ego. But whenever the number four disappears, we shall have the ninety-six pomegranates, the rich expression of the life of Christ in the open air.

pp. The Pillars Being Hollow
and Their Thickness Being Four Fingers

Jeremiah 52:21 says, "The thickness thereof was four fingers: it was hollow." Each pillar was a cylinder whose walls were four fingers thick, and within each pillar was a large hollow space. This signifies that God's building is of the human creature, represented by the number four, filled with the Spirit. Undoubtedly, the brass pillar is the condemned and judged human creature. Within the judged creature is an empty space that must be filled with an invisible reality. We should not be muddy, thin, and filled with sand, for then there would be no hollow space within. Rather, we must be brass, four fingers thick, and hollow. Then it will be possible for our hollow space to be filled with reality, the Spirit.

qq. The Two Pillars Measured with One Height
of Thirty-five Cubits with One Cubit Covered

Second Chronicles 3:15 says, "Also he made for the front of the house two pillars of thirty and five cubits long" (Heb.). The two pillars had a combined height of thirty-five cubits, with one cubit covered. In the last message I said that each of the standing boards in the tabernacle was one and a half cubits wide. These boards stood horizontally side by side. But with the pillars it is not only a matter of being horizontal, but also of being vertical. The pillars were measured vertically, with one standing above another. This indicates that God's building is not only horizontal, but also vertical with some part hidden. Although it is easy for two brothers to stand side by side, it is difficult for one brother to be under the other. It is also difficult to be above others. If the building is to be strong, it must be vertical. The more vertical it is, the more space there will be. We should not only stand side by side with one another, but also above one another. In order to stand side by side, there is no need of sacrifice or to have any part covered. But if we would stand vertically, there is the need for some part to be covered.

First Kings 7:15 says that each pillar was eighteen cubits high, but 2 Chronicles 3:15 indicates that the two pillars were thirty-five cubits long. According to 2 Chronicles 3:15, one cubit is missing. This cubit must have been covered and sacrificed. One reference book says that half a cubit went into each of the pedestals. I do not accept this explanation because the Bible does not say that the pillars had a pedestal or a base. Another reference book says that a cubit was lost in the joint to the capital. I believe this explanation to be correct. This means that in order to be vertical, there is the need of sacrifice. If you consider your experience, you will see that there is no sacrifice required to be side by side with others. But if you would be under someone, like the pillar under the capital, you must sacrifice. If you do not sacrifice, you cannot have anyone above you. You would either cast others away or leap over them. In order to let others be above you, you must give in and sacrifice a part of yourself. Sisters, you need to sacrifice so that someone can be above you. You should not only be measured horizontally but also vertically. Throughout the years, I have always been under someone. To be under others is to bear others and to be partly covered by them. It is by this sacrifice that we can have the vertical building.

rr. The Network and the Chainwork
on the Two Capitals Being Seven on Each

First Kings 7:17 says, "And nets of checkerwork, and wreaths of chainwork, for the capitals which were upon the top of the pillars; seven for the one capital, and seven for the other capital." Here we see that the network and the chainwork on the two capitals were seven on each. This indicates that all the complicated situations are temporal, not eternal. All the crossing, breaking, and suppressing are temporary, yet they are complete, for they are in the number seven. One day, all this will be over, and there will be no more checkerwork and chainwork. Instead of network and an entwined wreath, we shall have a golden crown.

ss. The Number Three Being Hidden

Notice that in these two pillars the number three is hidden. This indicates that the Triune God is hidden. That the pillars are twelve cubits in circumference and capitals four cubits in diameter implies the presence of the number three. The number three, the Triune God, is real but invisible. In every situation the Triune God is real, but He is hidden.

tt. The Brass, the Lily, and the Pomegranates All Being on the Two Pillars

The brass, the lily, and the pomegranates are all on the two pillars. This reveals that death, resurrection, and the expression of life are all a testimony in God's building. Today, we are here with this testimony. All these points are crucial, and I hope that you will spend time to pray and fellowship about them until they get into you and become your experience. Then we shall know what a pillar is and how we can become a pillar.

LIFE-STUDY OF GENESIS

MESSAGE EIGHTY-FIVE

THE BUILDER OF THE PILLARS—
THE SKILLFUL HIRAM

(1)

In this message, a parenthesis in our study of the pillars, we shall consider Hiram, the builder of the pillars (1 Kings 7:13-15). In 1 Kings and 2 Chronicles the Bible has much to say about Hiram. Although David and Solomon both prepared skillful men for the building of the temple, Hiram is the only one of these skillful builders mentioned by name. The Bible not only mentions Hiram's name, but also gives his background in a detailed and meaningful way, telling us of his mother and father and of Hiram himself. As we study the Bible, we must realize that it has no wasted words. Everything it stresses or repeats is meaningful. Instead of considering some verse as mere repetition, we must find the significance in each repetition.

When I spent much time studying the two pillars in 1 Kings 7 nearly fifty years ago, I did not see any light. I only saw that the names of the two pillars were Jachin, meaning, "He shall establish," and Boaz, meaning, "In it is strength." But as we have been considering Jacob's dream and his experience at Bethel, I began to study these two pillars again. This time a great deal of light, like the fourth-day light (1:14-19), shined upon me. In my study of the pillars I found that many verses mention Hiram, the builder of the pillars. I knew by the speaking of the Spirit within that I had to pay attention to this. While I was considering the pillars, light also came concerning Hiram's mother and father, neither of whom is named in the Scriptures. I was especially bothered by the fact that, according to the Hebrew text, 1 Kings 7:14 says that Hiram was of the tribe of Naphtali. As I considered all these things further, I realized that I needed one complete message to discharge my burden on the builder of the pillars.

When you hear about the builder of the pillars, you may say, "I don't think that I could ever be a builder. As long as God's mercy and grace would make me a pillar, I would be more than satisfied." But do not be so limited. God's grace is unlimited. It can not only make you a pillar, but even a builder of pillars. Although I am not saying that all of us will be pillars or builders of pillars, I believe that in the coming years many, even some sisters, will become pillars. If you do not believe this word now, I would ask you to wait for several years. Then you will see many pillars raised up in the Lord's recovery. When that time comes, I will be happy. Furthermore, I believe that a good number of us will also become Hirams, the builders of pillars. God needs these Hirams. Only one temple was built in Solomon's time, but today many local churches need to be built. How many Hirams will be required for this work! Every local church needs at least one Hiram. Whenever there is a Hiram in a local church, that church is in glory. Thank the Lord that He has raised up a number of Hirams in the past. But I believe that in the future the Lord will perfect many more Hirams.

I. HIS MOTHER BEING A WOMAN OF THE DAUGHTERS OF DAN

Let us now see the constituent, or the constitution, of a Hiram. We need to know the constitution of those who are builders, not of the building generally, but of the pillars specifically. Firstly, Hiram's mother was "a woman of the daughters of Dan" (2 Chron. 2:14). No one can tell whether Dan here refers to the tribe of Dan or to the city of Dan. Nonetheless, it is certain that it refers to people from Dan, for the city of Dan was also of the people of the tribe of Dan. Hiram's father was a Tyrian, a man of Tyre, a pagan country. Hence, Hiram's mother was from the holy land and his father from a pagan country. As strange as it seems, the Bible further says that Hiram himself was of the tribe of Naphtali (1 Kings 7:14, Heb.). Therefore, his mother was of Dan, his father was of Tyre, and he himself was of Naphtali. How could he be of the tribe of Naphtali, since his mother was of Dan and his father of Tyre? The Bible does not tell us. It is a secret. In the light of the New Testament we may apprehend the significance of this secret. The New Testament unveils to us that we were born a sinful and worldly man. But we have been regenerated and transformed to be a man in resurrection. To be a man in resurrection by being regenerated and transformed is to be transferred into the tribe of "Naphtali" and to no longer be of "Dan" or of "Tyre."

Let us take the example of an elder who has been transformed. An elder should not be a gentleman, but a transformed man. Although a certain elder is the son of a woman from "Dan" and of a man from "Tyre," he must be transferred into a person from the tribe of "Naphtali." In the church life the tribe of "Naphtali" is the tribe of transformation. Once we are in the tribe of "Naphtali," we are no longer the same as our "Danite" mother and our "Tyrian" father. You may think it is too much to say that Naphtali may be interpreted as the tribe of transformation. But read on, and surely you will be convinced that this is so. Among the twelve tribes, only one tribe, the tribe of Naphtali, is the tribe of transformation. Judah is the tribe of kingship, Levi of priesthood, and Joseph of the double portion. Naphtali is the tribe of resurrection. To be in resurrection means to be in transformation.

The tribe of Dan is the tribe of idolatry that caused God's people to stumble and fall from God's way. Genesis 49:17 says, "Dan shall be a serpent by the way, an adder in the path, that biteth the horse heels, so that his rider shall fall backward." According to Judges 18, this is exactly what the Danites did. They took Micah's images which he had in his house and the priest whom Micah had hired to serve in his house. Judges 18:31 says, "They set them up Micah's graven image, which he made." This was the greatest stumbling to the children of Israel; it was the biting of the adder that caused the rider to fall backward. Furthermore, Jeroboam, the king of the northern tribes, set up golden calves in Bethel and in Dan to cause the children of God to stumble (1 Kings 12:28-30). Due to this, in 1 Chronicles 2 through 9, where all the other tribes of Israel are mentioned in detail, there is no mention of Dan. In these chapters Dan is cut off from the record of God's people. Moreover, in Revelation 7, where we have the sealing of the children of Israel, there is no mention of the tribe of Dan.

Let us consider further some details relating to the tribe of Dan. Genesis 49:17 says that Dan was "a serpent by the way, an adder in the path." Dan was an adder, a poisonous snake, biting the horse's heels, "so that his rider shall fall backward." In the race of God's economy, this adder bites the horse and causes the rider to fall backward. This word in 49:17 was not spoken by a slanderer; it was uttered by Jacob as part of his blessing of his sons. When it was time to bestow his blessing upon Dan, Jacob had to be faithful to God's inspiration. Immediately after speaking the words recorded in 49:17, Jacob said, "I have waited for thy salvation, O Lord." This means, "Lord, save me from this serpent, this adder." In 49:16 Jacob said, "Dan shall judge his people, as one of the tribes of Israel." Here, Jacob was praying that Dan might continue as a tribe. This indicated that he was in danger of being omitted. Hence, his father's prayer was also a prediction. God heard this prayer. In the book of Ezekiel we see that in the coming millennium the tribe of Dan will be recovered (Ezek. 48:1).

These details concerning Dan indicate that to be a mother who is "a woman of the daughters of Dan" is to be a mother in sin. All our mothers are mothers in sin. In Psalm 51:5 David said, "In sin did my mother conceive me." The fact that Hiram's mother was of Dan indicates that his origin, like ours, was of sin. Even the Apostle Paul said that he was the foremost of sinners (1 Tim. 1:15). Spiritually speaking, in God's eyes Paul's mother was also a "daughter of Dan." We all must confess that our mothers are also those of "Dan." If you would become a builder of pillars, you must firstly admit that you are a person born in sin. We may seem to be nice, humble, kind, gentle, and pure; but because our mother is of "the daughters of Dan," our origin by birth is the origin of the serpent. In Matthew 23:33 the Lord Jesus addressed the religious ones as "serpents" and a "brood of vipers." If you were to say to me, "Brother Lee, you are no good; you are a generation of vipers," I would nod my head in agreement. In us, that is, in our flesh, nothing good dwells (Rom. 7:18). We all must recognize what our origin is. Our origin is that of a woman from the tribe of "Dan," the tribe of an adder biting the horse's heels and causing the rider to fall backward from God's economy.

II. HIS FATHER BEING A TYRIAN

Hiram's father was a Tyrian, a man of Tyre (1 Kings 7:14). According to Ezekiel 28, Tyre was a place filled with commerce (Ezek. 28:16). Tyre was a commercial center, a place of international trade, like today's Hong Kong. Because Tyre was filled with merchandise, she was one with Satan (Ezek. 28:12). Ezekiel 28 reveals that the king of Tyre was one with Satan and even the very embodiment of Satan. Where commerce is, there Satan is also, for Satan is in commerce. If you would see Satan today, go to the commercial city of Hong Kong.

III. THE MARRIAGE OF HIS PARENTS BEING AGAINST GOD'S HOLY REGULATION

The marriage of Hiram's parents was against God's holy regulation (Deut. 7:3). A woman of the tribe of the serpent married a man from the country of Satan. What a combination! This woman of the tribe of the serpent married a man from the country of Tyre because of riches, commerce.

Not only in Hiram's day but today also you need skill to make money. For this reason there are many technical colleges in the United States. These technical schools teach skills, techniques, and trades that enable people to earn money. The only goal of colleges and universities is to train people to be money makers.

I would encourage you all to learn how to make money. I have encouraged my grandchildren to study medicine. Although some saints have tried to discourage them from studying medicine, telling them that they only need to read the Bible and love the Lord, I have said, "Don't listen to this talk. Those who say this don't know life. You must listen to your grandfather. He knows life better than you all. Go to study medicine." One of my grandsons took my word and earned all A's in his first year of pre-medical studies. Do not think that this is a kind of love for the world. As you shall see, I have a definite purpose in doing this. Hiram became the builder of the pillars. But if his father had not been a Tyrian, he would not have had the skill to fashion the pillars. We all were born of a "Danite" mother and we all need a "Tyrian" father. The more of a "Tyrian" our father is, the better. If you think that I am too extreme in saying this, I would ask you to read this message to the end.

IV. BECOMING ONE OF THE TRIBE OF NAPHTALI

According to the Hebrew text of 1 Kings 7:14, we are also told that Hiram was of the tribe of Naphtali. Although his mother was a Danite and his father a Tyrian, Hiram eventually became one belonging to the tribe of Naphtali.

A. A Hind Set Free

In 49:21 Jacob said, "Naphtali is a hind let loose: he giveth beautiful words" (Heb.). Here Jacob spoke of Naphtali with high favor. A hind does not seem to be related to beautiful words. But we must not understand the Bible according to our natural mind; we must understand the Bible according to the Bible.

1. Trusting and Rejoicing in God

A hind signifies a person who trusts in God in a desperate situation. Habakkuk 3:17 and 18 say, "Although the fig tree shall not blossom, neither shall fruit be in the vine; the labour of the olive shall fail, and the fields shall yield no food; the flock shall be cut off from the fold, and there shall be no herd in the stalls: Yet I will rejoice in the Lord, and I will joy in the God of my salvation" (Heb.). Those who trust in God and rejoice in God in the midst of a desperate situation, a situation in which every source of supply is cut off, are hinds.

2. Walking Upon High Places

Habakkuk 3:19 says, "The Lord God is my strength, and he will make my feet like hinds' feet, and he will make me to walk upon mine high places." Those who trust in God walk, not in the valleys, but upon the tops of the mountains. If you do not know how to exercise faith in God when you are in a desperate situation, at that time you will creep in the valleys. You will never walk and skip upon the mountains. Only those who trust in God when they are in a desperate situation can leap upon the mountaintops. People may say, "Look! The fig tree does not blossom, the vine does not bear fruit, the olive labors in vain, the fields yield no food, the flocks are cut off in the fold, and there is no herd in the stalls. Oh, the situation is desperate, and we are finished!" When you hear this, you should say, "Praise the Lord! Now is the time for me to trust in Him." If you are like this, you will not be discouraged. Rather, you will leap and skip like a hind upon the mountaintops.

3. Living in Resurrection

The hind is also mentioned in the title of Psalm 22, which says, "Upon the tune of the hind of the morning" (Heb.). This psalm is about Christ in resurrection through crucifixion. The first verse was uttered by the Lord Jesus on the cross: "My God, my God, why hast thou forsaken me?" However, verse 22 says, "I will declare thy name unto my brethren: in the midst of the assembly will I praise thee" (Heb.). This verse is quoted in Hebrews 2:12, which relates the resurrected Christ to the church. Hence, Psalm 22, sung to the tune of the hind of the morning, is on Christ in resurrection for the church. In the Old Testament the hind refers not only to a person who trusts in God and walks upon the mountaintops, but also to one who lives in resurrection for God's assembly, for the church life.

Are you a "hind," or are you a "turtle"? I never saw a turtle skipping upon the mountaintops. Turtles are found in low places near water. Those who trust in God are not "turtles" but "hinds." They are in resurrection for God's assembly, the church. Only by regeneration and transformation can we be this kind of person. Naphtali is the tribe of the hind, and a hind signifies a regenerated and transformed person, a person who trusts in God, walks on the mountaintops, and lives in resurrection for the church life. How wonderful!

B. Giving Beautiful Words

Naphtali also gives beautiful words. Naphtali was in the land of Galilee (Matt. 4:15). All the first group of apostles came from Galilee, and in Acts 1:11 they were addressed as "men, Galileans." Out from these Galileans, people of Naphtali, came beautiful words, that is, the preaching of the gospel. In the New Testament we see that the word which came out of these Galileans was the word of life (Acts 5:20), the word of grace (Acts 14:3), the word of salvation (Acts 13:26), the word of wisdom (1 Cor. 12:8), the word of knowledge (1 Cor. 12:8), and the word of building (Acts 20:32).

V. HIS TYRIAN FATHER DYING AND HIS DANITE MOTHER BECOMING WIDOWED

The Apostle Paul was truly a Hiram. I do not know who Paul's mother was, but, spiritually speaking, I am certain that she was a "daughter of Dan," a daughter of the tribe of the serpent. Undoubtedly, in principle, Paul's father was a "Tyrian." Paul was brought up "at the feet of Gamaliel" (Acts 22:3), a doctor of the law. At that time, law was the highest science among the Jews, and whoever became a doctor of law was considered to be most outstanding. Gamaliel taught Paul everything regarding the religion of their forefathers. Paul's studying under Gamaliel was equivalent to studying in a seminary today. Although a seminary does not teach a trade and thus is different from a technical college, the principle of both a seminary and a technical college is the same in teaching knowledge.

Consider also the example of Moses. Moses was born of a Jewish mother, but he was brought up in the royal family in Egypt. Acts 7:22 says, "Moses was trained in all the wisdom of the Egyptians, and he was powerful in his words and deeds." He was a scholar in Egypt. Paul was a scholar of religious knowledge, and Moses was a scholar of secular knowledge. However, again the principle was the same. Eventually, both Moses and Paul became pillar builders. In 1 Corinthians 3:10 Paul said that he was "a wise masterbuilder." Both Moses and Paul had a "Danite" mother and a "Tyrian" father.

The royal Egyptian family was Moses' "Tyrian" father, for it was there that he learned all the wisdom of Egypt. This was the source of his Egyptian skill. The teaching of Gamaliel was the source of Paul's knowledge. In this way, Gamaliel became Paul's "Tyrian" father.

Now we must see a crucial point: All the "Tyrian" fathers must die. Hiram learned his trade from his Tyrian father, but eventually this Tyrian father died. As far as Moses was concerned, the royal family of Egypt died and was cut off. After Moses had learned everything of the Egyptians, that Egyptian source was terminated. Likewise, after Paul had learned everything from Gamaliel, the source of Gamaliel was cut off. In like manner, we all must be sons of a widow. Our father must die, but our mother may remain as a widow. Our Egyptian father or our Gamaliel must die, leaving us as the sons of a widowed mother. This means that the source of our secular or religious skill must die, but that the source of our human being must still exist. Today, we all must have a deceased father and a widowed mother.

In Moses' time, no one could have understood God's plan for the tabernacle like he could, because no one else had gained all the wisdom of the Egyptians. Moses acquired the wisdom of the Egyptians before he was forty years of age. After gaining it, he thought that he was qualified to deliver his people out of the hands of the Egyptians (Acts 7:23-25), but he failed in this endeavor. After Moses fled from Egypt, he lived in the wilderness for forty years. By the time he was eighty years of age, he considered himself to be a dead man. In his Psalm, Psalm 90, Moses said that people may expect to live to be seventy, and that the stronger ones may live to be eighty (v. 10). When Moses was eighty years old, he might have said to himself, "I am finished. What can I do? Forty years ago I could have done something, but I cannot do anything today. I am not yet dead, but I am dying." As Moses was dying there in the wilderness, he one day saw the burning bush (Exo. 3:2). Although the bush was burning, it was not consumed. In the vision of the burning bush God seemed to be telling Moses, "Moses, I will make you burning, but I will not burn you. I don't need you to be the fuel. When you were forty years of age, you had a great deal of fuel, but now you are old, dried up, and have no more fuel. I have come to make you burning." At the time of this vision, Moses' "Tyrian" father had finally died. Later, as Moses led the children of Israel in the wilderness, what he had learned in the royal palace became useful. Because no one else had all the wisdom of the Egyptians, no one else could have done the work he did in the wilderness.

The principle is the same with a brother who has gained a great deal of Bible knowledge in the past. This knowledge of the Bible is his "Tyrian" father. But this "Tyrian" father must die. The source of his Bible knowledge must be terminated. Then whatever he has learned in the past will become useful in resurrection, and he will be able to deliver a word as few others are able to do. Just as the wisdom of the Egyptians became useful in the resurrected Moses, so whatever we learn in college, seminary, or Bible school will become useful in resurrection. However, if our "Tyrian" father still lives and we remain in the natural life, the "Tyrian" skill will be of no avail to the building up of God's temple.

I encourage all the young people to get a college degree. Do not make spirituality an excuse for not studying. Rather, study more diligently than the secular students, get the highest grades, and go on for advanced degrees. Do not stop with one Ph.D., but get two or three Ph.D.'s. Also learn to speak a number of other languages. Gain the "Tyrian" skills and the "Egyptian" knowledge. Become a doctor in biology, medicine, or nuclear physics. But then let the "Tyrian" father die. I have told you how I encouraged my grandson to study medicine. Now I will tell you what is truly on my heart. After he finishes medical school, I will say, "Forget about being a doctor and use your medical training to interpret the Bible." His medical training will make him very useful. Young people, gain all the up-to-date knowledge, graduate from college, and then say goodbye to your "Tyrian" father. Graduate from seminary and then say, "Seminary, thank you and goodbye. I have nothing more to do with you, but I will use the skill I have gained from you."

Young people, you all must study. Do not use the three

weekly life-study messages as an excuse. You must both study earnestly and read the life-study messages. Otherwise, I would have no trust in you because the Lord would put no trust in you. You must acquire the "Tyrian" knowledge and graduate from the "University of Tyre." But after you gain your "Tyrian" education, you must put your "Tyrian" father in a coffin and bury him, so that your "Danite" mother becomes a widow. Then you will be of the tribe of Naphtali, useful in resurrection for God's building.

Some may ask me about the Apostles Peter and John, pointing out that they had no higher education and that in Acts 4:13 they were described as "uneducated and unlearned men." This, of course, is true. But who was the leading pillar builder in the New Testament? Undoubtedly, it was Paul. Peter wrote just two Epistles, but Paul wrote fourteen Epistles. Peter even recognized his shortage by recommending Paul's writings, saying, "Our beloved brother Paul, according to the wisdom given to him, wrote to you" (2 Pet. 3:15). Peter even confessed that some of Paul's writings were difficult to understand (2 Pet. 3:16). Peter seemed to be saying, "You must read Paul's writings to learn something deeper than I can give you." We need Peters today, but we also need Pauls, those who can write more epistles. Some may still say, "How about the Apostle John? Didn't he write a gospel containing twenty-one chapters and the book of Revelation containing twenty-two chapters?" John's "Tyrian" education only enabled him to do this much; he could not do what Paul was able to do. John could say, "In the beginning was the Word," "In Him was life, and the life was the light of men," and "Behold, the Lamb of God." John could tell people that if they believed in Him, they would have life, but that if they did not believe in Him, they would die. But John was not able to write Romans chapters four or seven or the book of Ephesians. If John had been asked to do this, he might have said, "I am not able to do it. Go to Brother Paul." John was qualified to see the vision of the great harlot and of the New Jerusalem, but he was not the one to write books like Romans, Ephesians, and Hebrews.

There is a need in the Lord's recovery today for those with the highest education. Young people, you must endeavor to gain the best education. Arrange your daily schedule in this way: seven and a half hours for sleep, one and a half hours for eating, one hour for exercise, eight hours for study, and six hours for spiritual things. If you expend your energy in this way, by the time you are thirty you will be able to begin your ministry like the Lord Jesus did (Luke 3:23). Continue your studies until you are thirty. If many take this way, we shall have no shortage of pillar makers.

Do not get married too soon. I do not like to see the brothers getting married before the age of twenty-five. Do not be burdened down too soon with marriage and children. Rather, use your time and energy for studying. The age of twenty-six is soon enough for brothers to begin having children. Furthermore, I do not like to see the sisters getting married before the age of twenty-two. If the sisters marry too early and have children too soon, they may be overburdened and even spoiled. Follow the schedule I recommend until you are twenty-five years old and see what will be the issue. This surely is good for God's recovery.

Are you anxious to be a Hiram? If you are, then you must be related to your "Tyrian" father, learn the "Tyrian" skill and trade, and gain the wisdom of the "Egyptians." Do not stop your schooling too soon. You should get a master's degree, or preferably a Ph.D. All the church people must be learned ones. We are neither ignorant nor undereducated. Rather, we would have the highest education. We would acquire all the wisdom of the "Egyptians," but we would not work for the "Egyptians"—we would work for the holy tabernacle. We should be able to say, "I know medicine and nuclear science, but I am not working for that. I am working for the building up of the church. I have learned a trade, but I am not occupied with this. I am building the pillars for the temple of my God." For this, our "Tyrian" father must die, our "Danite" mother must be widowed, and we must belong to the tribe of "Naphtali," the tribe of transformation. Be a person full of learning, but do not use your learning for secular business. Use it fully for the Lord's building work. Your life and your being must not only be transformed but also transferred. You must no longer be of "Dan" or of "Tyre," but absolutely of

"Naphtali." As hinds that have been freed, we would trust in God, walk upon the mountaintops, and live in resurrection for the church life, giving forth words of life, grace, salvation, wisdom, knowledge, and building. If we are like this, then we shall be builders of pillars.

LIFE-STUDY OF GENESIS

MESSAGE EIGHTY-SIX

THE BUILDER OF THE PILLARS—
THE SKILLFUL HIRAM

(2)

In this message we shall consider further the builder of the pillars, the skillful Hiram (1 Kings 7:13-14; 2 Chron. 2:13-14).

It is not easy to know the Bible. Sometimes when translators have difficulty with a particular passage, they assume that the manuscripts are in error. However, when we probe into the depths of the revelation of the Bible, we must worship God. Often what at first glance appears to be a mistake in the manuscripts turns out to be a mysterious truth hidden in the Scriptures. This is true with respect to 1 Kings 7:14. The King James Version renders the verse as, "He [Hiram] was a widow's son of the tribe of Naphtali." According to this rendering and the understanding of most translators, the modifier, "of the tribe of Naphtali," goes with the word "widow." This would mean that this verse says that the widow was of the tribe of Naphtali. But 2 Chronicles 2:14 says that Hiram was "the son of a woman of the daughters of Dan." How could a daughter of Dan also be of the tribe of Naphtali? Some translators, neglecting the Hebrew text of 1 Kings 7:14, tried their best to reconcile this discrepancy, but they failed. By studying the Hebrew text we have learned that this verse should be translated as follows: "The son of a widowed woman; and he was of the tribe of Naphtali." Thus, Hiram, the son, was of the tribe of Naphtali. This solves the problem.

In this record of Hiram, the pillar builder, we have three peoples: the people of Dan, the people of Tyre, and the people of Naphtali. Hiram's mother was of Dan, his father was of Tyre, and he himself became one of the tribe of Naphtali. We do not know how a man whose mother was of Dan and whose father was of Tyre could be of the tribe of Naphtali. We only know that the Bible tells us so.

VI. HIRAM'S TRANSFER TO THE TRIBE OF NAPHTALI BEING MYSTERIOUS

The Bible is profound, and many things revealed in it are mysterious. Although there seems to be no reason for Hiram to be of the tribe of Naphtali, the Bible clearly tells that he was of this tribe. If we consider the significance of Dan, Tyre, and Naphtali, we shall worship God. Dan was a people of the serpent that bit the horse in the race of God (Gen. 49:17), and Tyre, a center filled with commerce, was related to Satan (Ezek. 28:12, 16). How marvelous that a man born of a woman of the people of the serpent and of a man of the people related to Satan could eventually become one of the tribe of Naphtali.

Naphtali is a hind (Gen. 49:21), which is useful to God. The description of the hind in the Old Testament record is very significant. According to the Bible, a hind signifies a person who trusts in God when he is in a desperate situation. Due to this trust, the Lord causes him to walk, even to skip, upon the high places (Hab. 3:17-19). The title of Psalm 22 reveals that the hind also signifies the very Christ who, having passed through the suffering of crucifixion, has entered into resurrection for the sake of the church. Hebrews 2:11 and 12 reveal that the resurrected Christ is for the church. Therefore, the hind signifies a person who trusts in God, who walks upon the mountaintops, and who lives by the resurrected Christ for God's building.

Which do you prefer to be—a serpent, a "Tyrian," or a hind? I certainly prefer to be one of the tribe of Naphtali, trusting in God, walking upon the high places, and living in the resurrected Christ for God's building. Hiram was such a person.

When some read this, they may think that it is merely allegorization or inference. It is not wrong to make inferences. If we see the letters b-o-y, we may rightly infer that they spell the word "boy." This inference is not only correct, but also necessary. In order to make inferences related to what is found in the Bible, we must firstly know the Bible. Many who do not know the significance of the tribe of Dan or of the country of Tyre would say, "Dan is Dan and Tyre is Tyre. We don't care for all these things." Genesis 49:21 says, "Naphtali is a hind let loose: he giveth beautiful words" (Heb.). Perhaps you have never paid attention to this verse. Naphtali is a hind that is released and freed. This hind knows no bondage and is not held in any fold; rather, it is freed to skip on the mountaintops. We must be such persons, persons who are freed from every bondage and man-made fold.

Now we must ask how a man born of a Danite mother and a Tyrian father could become one of the tribe of Naphtali. It is mysterious. A portion of the personal history of every Christian should be mysterious. Every Christian has a mysterious history. When I was young, I enjoyed playing soccer. I could play soccer all day long. But when I went to play again after I was saved, a strange thing happened. As I waited for the ball to come my way, I found that my feet would not move. When the ball did come to me, I simply could not play. Formerly, I was the fastest one in running and carrying the ball, but now I could not move and I eventually withdrew from the game. Others were shocked, and some said, "What happened?" I answered, "It is difficult for me to say." This is mysterious. Have you not had mysterious experiences like this? If not, then I doubt that you are my brother or sister in the Lord. Although I was a natural born soccer player, I suddenly became another person. For about fifty-five years I have not returned to play soccer.

There is a mysterious element in our regenerated life. Yes, we were born of a "Danite" mother and of a "Tyrian" father, but we have been regenerated to be another person. Even the young ones among us can testify that certain mysterious things have happened to them. Part of their human history is mysterious. The more you take this way, the more mysterious you will become. My wife has to admit that many times she cannot understand me. On occasion, something causes anger to rise up in me, but a few minutes later I begin to say, "O Lord Jesus! Praise the Lord! Amen!" Although my wife exercises her ability to understand what is going on within me, she simply cannot fathom what happens to me. Because this is so mysterious, I can only say, "Praise the Lord!" How mysterious this is!

Both Dan and Tyre are visible, but Naphtali is invisible. People could see that I was born of my natural mother and father, but they could not see how I became such a mysterious person. Every spiritual "Naphtalite" is invisible and mysterious. People should not be entirely able to understand you. If your classmates in school can understand everything about you, you are finished. You are not a wonderful Christian, for a wonderful Christian should not be that understandable. Instead, you should be a puzzle to your classmates or those with whom you work. You must also be a mysterious person in your married life. Although your dear wife may be a good sister, you should be somewhat mysterious in her eyes. If you are not mysterious, I do not believe that you are a good brother. The sisters should likewise be somewhat mysterious to their husbands. Before the Lord, I can testify that I do not understand certain things about my wife. She should not be able to bear so much, but due to the mysterious life within her she is able to bear much more than I think. We Christians have a mysterious source and origin. We even have a mysterious Originator within us.

It is a secret to us how Hiram became one of the tribe of Naphtali. We must bow our heads and worship God for this mysterious element concealed in Hiram's history. How marvelous that his history not only records that his mother was of the tribe of the serpent and that his father was of the nation of commerce, a country related to Satan, but that he became one of the tribe of Naphtali. Hence, his history implies a mysterious part of his life that was used by God for His building. Although in the Bible the reason for this point is not mentioned, according to our experience we can understand that this is the mysterious part of our Christian life. The greater this mysterious portion is, the better, because it is this part that made Hiram one of the tribe of Naphtali and that made him the builder of pillars. Likewise, it is this mysterious part that makes us good for God's building. We should not live as one born of "Dan" or of "Tyre." Rather, we must live as one who has been transferred into the tribe of Naphtali. Hallelujah! Today, I am not of "Dan" or of "Tyre"—I am of the tribe of "Naphtali."

VII. THE TYRIAN FATHER, THE SOURCE OF SECULAR SKILL, HAVING TO DIE THAT THE SON WHO LEARNED THIS SKILL THROUGH THE WORLDLY FATHER MAY BE RELEASED FROM THE WORLDLY TIE

Hiram's Tyrian father died. What a difference there would have been if his mother had died instead of his father! If that had been the case, this record would not match our experience, and it would be impossible to allegorize this portion of the Word. Praise the Lord that our "father," not our "mother," has died. This means that the source of secular skill has been cut off by God. The father signifies the source of skill, and the mother signifies human existence. If our "mother" died and our "father" lived, we would be "ghosts" fully involved with the world. We must go on existing as humans. Even Paul says, "I have been crucified with Christ, and it is no longer I who live" (Gal. 2:20). The old man, the old "father," has been crucified; yet we still exist. That "I" who continues to exist is the "mother" of our human existence.

Moses is a good example. He was raised in the royal Egyptian family where he learned all the wisdom of the Egyptians. At the age of forty, he considered himself qualified to deliver his people from the usurping hand of the Egyptians. However, he failed because his "Tyrian" father, his connection with Egypt, still remained. This indicated that the source of his skill had not been cut off. The Lord intervened to break that connection, and Moses fled to the wilderness. Although Moses' "Tyrian" father, the royal Egyptian family, died, he himself continued to exist. The widowed "mother" remained. Although she continued to live, she was no longer tied to her husband.

Let us now apply this to our own experience. You may earn a Ph.D. from Massachusetts Institute of Technology. But after you earn this degree, Massachusetts Institute of Technology must die. This does not mean that you must die. You must continue to exist, but your existence must be widowed, separated from the worldly source. You continue to possess your skill, but the origin and source of that skill has been cut off. Your continued existence is the "mother," and the source of your skill, which has been cut off, is your deceased "father." Now you possess the skill without the source, and your human existence is no longer tied to your worldly origin.

Many of the young brothers and sisters are unbalanced and say, "We are in the Lord's recovery and we are expecting the Lord to come back soon. He may come back in two years. Why then should we worry about finishing high school and preparing ourselves for college? We should spend our time to pray-read and to fellowship with other brothers and sisters. Since the Lord is coming soon, why should we waste our time reading and studying?" If this is your attitude, the Lord may delay His coming back until you have learned to study. Actually, you should not just aim to finish high school, but also to graduate from college, and even to earn a Ph.D. I know what is on the heart of the young people. Many sisters think that it is sufficient to graduate from high school or, at most, junior college. They may say, "We sisters will not be elders. Why should we waste our time in school? Isn't it good enough to learn to type and make six hundred dollars a month? Let us enjoy an easy Christian life and a happy church life." Sisters, you must abandon this concept. No matter how much you love the Lord, if you hold this concept, you will never be very useful to Him. No time spent in studying is wasted. As young people, you must use your time to study. Although the Lord may come back in a few years, you must still study and learn the "Tyrian" skill. If you are under the age of twenty-three, your time must be devoted to your education. You should finish your university course by the age of twenty-two or twenty-three. This is not a regulation of the church in the Lord's recovery; this is my teaching. From now on, when young brothers and sisters come to me, I shall ask them what year they have finished in school. If anyone aged twenty-two would say that he has not yet graduated from high school, I would not waste my time in talking to him. Such a person, four years behind in school, might be unable to understand my fellowship concerning the Bible. But if a brother would tell me that he has just finished his first year of graduate school, I would be happy to talk with him concerning the depths of the Bible.

Although you should do your best to earn an advanced degree, after you have earned it, you must be prepared to sever the worldly ties. Do not burn your diploma (you will need that for business purposes), but say within yourself, "My 'Tyrian' father has died. The day of my graduation will be the day of his funeral." After you have labored for years to earn your degree, you must put your "Tyrian" father in a coffin and bury him. Never boast that you have graduated from a university. After Moses left the royal Egyptian family, he never mentioned it again. That family was buried. But many Christians with earned doctorates always like to put the title "Dr." in front of their names. Fifty or sixty years ago, people liked to say that they had graduated from Oxford or Cambridge. Although some boast of their education, after we have earned our degrees, we must bury Cambridge, Oxford, and every other university. The father of our "Tyrian" skill must die and be buried. The skill is useful, but the father has a foul odor.

As you read this, you may say that you do not understand what I am talking about. This is mysterious, and there is no need to understand it. The best Christians are those who study diligently and who afterwards seem to forget that they have earned a degree. Their unbelieving relatives and friends will not understand this. To them, it is mysterious that we would devote so much time and labor to earn a degree and then not respect it. Praise the Lord that they do not understand us! This is another aspect of our Christian mystery. We Christians have many mysterious aspects. For example, I know of some Christians who freely spend money on others, but not on themselves. Their relatives do not understand why they are so strict with themselves and so generous with others. We Christians must be people with a mysterious history. How mysterious of us to earn a degree and then to cut off our "Tyrian" father!

If this father does not die, he will bind us to the world, and our education will become the strongest tie. In my ministry throughout the years I have learned that no highly educated person can understand the Bible unless he cuts off this worldly tie. Being proud of your education will hinder you from knowing the Scriptures. No matter how educated you are, you must humbly tell the Lord that you are a teachable little child and that in your whole being you are utterly empty. You should be able to say, "Lord, although I have three Ph.D.'s, I know nothing. I am not filled up by my education. I am empty in my spirit, in my mind, and in my whole being." Many highly educated professional people are filled to the brim. For this reason, even after they are saved, they are unable to receive anything from the Word. Their pride has usurped them. We need to cut the tie with our "Tyrian" father and become like a child who knows nothing. Although we have knowledge, we would not be proud or filled with knowledge; instead, we would be empty. If we are like this, we shall be able to understand the Bible.

We need some brothers and sisters with doctor's degrees. It would be very beneficial to have some with Ph.D.'s in biblical Hebrew and Greek. It would also be helpful for some to earn Ph.D.'s in space science and nuclear physics. The church should not be poor or on a low level. Rather, it should have the highest people on earth. Young people, this must become your burden.

VIII. THE DANITE MOTHER, SIGNIFYING HUMAN EXISTENCE, REMAINING AS A WIDOW

Although the "Tyrian" father must die, the "Danite" mother, our human existence, must remain as a widow. Young people, if you take this word, after a number of years you will be able to say, "Lord, I thank You for that word about the 'Tyrian' father and 'Danite' mother. I have earned a doctor's degree, and the father of this degree has died, but the 'Danite' mother still lives. As the son of this widowed mother, I still possess my skills." If you are like this, you will certainly be useful in the Lord's hand.

Although we believe that the Lord is coming soon, we should still expect to have a long life on the earth for the Lord's use. In my early ministry I repeatedly prayed Solomon's prayer for wisdom in coming in and going out among

God's people (1 Kings 3:7, 9). I can testify that the Lord has answered my prayer, helping me learn how to behave in the house of God and how to come in and go out among the saints. In addition, I have often prayed that the Lord would give me long life. I do not want to learn the things of God and then die shortly afterwards. Rather, I want to live a long life so that everything I have learned may be useful. All the young people should have this attitude and say, "Lord, I know You are coming soon. But I don't want to see You in resurrection—I want to see You in rapture. I want to live a long life until You come, not that I might have enjoyment, but that I might be useful for Your purpose on earth."

When my mother died in 1945, I wept. Although I have undergone many sufferings in the thirty-two years since then, I have hardly wept at all in these years. However, when in 1972 the news came to me that Brother Nee had died, I wept. I wept because I knew him intimately, had spent many years with him, and had received great help from him for the Lord's recovery. Year after year, he saw new things and had new experiences. Nearly everything he learned he passed on to me. From 1952 until he went to the Lord in 1972, he was in prison. I am sure that during those twenty years he learned many things, but not one word came out. This was the real reason I wept. How different the situation would be today if Brother Nee were still alive among us. Although I thank the Lord for those who are bearing the ark with me, I nevertheless constantly have a deep feeling of loneliness. If Brother Nee and my other senior co-workers were still living, I would not have this feeling. When I was with them on mainland China, I had some more experienced ones with whom I could have fellowship. I could refer matters to them, and they would always render me the help I needed. But when I refer matters to the brothers today, I feel that I am alone. I hope that in the coming years all of you will have many others with you on your level.

That the "Tyrian" father must die and our mother must keep on living means that we should ask the Lord to give us a long life. We should say, "Lord, I don't want to die early. I want to live to be eighty or ninety. If You do not come then, I am willing to die. But I still prefer to live until You come." We all, especially the young people, should pray like this.

The Lord has been merciful in answering my prayers for long life. But do not think that I have never had any diseases or illnesses. I have had a stomach ulcer, and it took me two and one half years to recover from a serious case of tuberculosis of the lungs. In order for our human existence to remain, we must stand against any weakness. Tell the Lord that you do not want to have a weak, unhealthy body. Do not think a spiritual person must be physically weak. Do not hold the concept that only by being physically weak can you learn to trust in the Lord. This concept is too spiritual. If you are too spiritual, you are not truly spiritual at all. Rather, you should say, "Lord, I don't agree with having an unhealthy body. Grant me a good appetite, the proper digestion, and the best sleep. Lord, promise me, as you have promised others, that my strength would be as my days. Every day must be filled with strength. I don't want to spend one day lying idly in bed. I refuse that kind of existence. I want to have a strong, healthy existence that is useful for Your purpose."

In addition to praying in this manner, you must also learn to take proper care of your body. Do not be unwise in your eating. The Lord has given me a good wife who exercises control over my eating. If it were not for her, I would take every opportunity to eat dessert. But because of her concern for my diet, I am healthy today. Daily, I eat the most healthy foods. Do not commit gradual suicide over a period of years by eating unwisely, but learn to keep yourself healthy. Take care of your body that your widowed "Danite" mother may go on living. Our purpose in this is not our health, but our being useful to the Lord.

In spite of the opposition, rumors, and criticisms, the Lord is opening doors throughout the country. He has given us an open door that no one is able to shut. But we are short of pillars. Recently, we have heard testimonies of what the Lord is doing in various places. However, we do not have the pillars to match the Lord's move. Doors are also opening in Europe, but there are not enough pillars. We must admit that we are short of pillars. This lack is due to the past situation. But, beginning now, we must cut off our past and go on. The young people must arise and tell the whole universe that the past situation is over. Young people, speak to the Lord, saying, "We young people have no history. We all will rise up. Lord, be merciful to us and do everything You can in the next several years to make us all pillars." This is my burden. I long to see that after some years many young ones will be ready to be sent out. If we had two strong pillars to go to one of the new places, within a few months three other localities would open up. The open doors always multiply like this. We go to one place, and our going there opens up other places. It all depends upon the pillars.

Most of the older ones among us have wasted many years. All the years spent sitting in Christianity have been wasted. Year after year went by, but everything remained the same. Our young people must not be like this. Even one month must make a difference. Nevertheless, the older brothers and sisters should not be disappointed. It is not too late for them to go on. There is a great need for those who can shepherd others. We all must endeavor to become useful.

I am certain that the way we are now taking is absolutely right. Do not consider any other way—dive into this flow and stay in it. Use this opportunity to learn, to be trained, to be adjusted, to be saturated by the Lord, and to be made useful for Him. We all must learn this way and never return to the old way.

I hate the old way. According to the old way, many go to the meetings clinging to their opinions and thinking that they are so experienced. When the brothers minister the Word, they "discern" the message (actually they are being critical), wanting to determine whether or not the brothers are scriptural. It is not your responsibility to discern the brothers. Let the Lord take care of that. Instead, you must learn your own lessons and have all the dealings necessary to make you useful. We all should hold this attitude. Do not think that you are too old to be useful. Everyone who wants to be useful can become useful.

This is not a doctrine; it is my practical fellowship with you all, especially with the young ones. Young people, I hope that your whole being will be open so that you may make a clear decision and say, "Lord, this is it. From now on, I will do everything possible to learn all I need to learn. Lord, I ask You to help me in this matter. After I graduate, my 'Tyrian' father must die, but my 'Danite' mother must continue to exist. Lord, grant me this kind of living that I may be useful to You."

IX. THE SECULAR SKILL BEING USEFUL FOR GOD'S BUILDING ONLY IN RESURRECTION AFTER THE WORLDLY FATHER HAS DIED AND THE LEARNED SON HAS BEEN TRANSFERRED TO THE TRIBE OF NAPHTALI

The secular skills we gain will only be useful for God's building in resurrection, that is, after the worldly father has died and we have been transferred into the tribe of Naphtali. After your "Tyrian" father has died and your "Danite" mother has become widowed, you must not remain a natural person. Anything natural is a waste. Instead of being natural, we must exercise ourselves to be in resurrection in every aspect of our living. This is a great matter. The more you exercise yourself to be in resurrection, the more useful you will be. You must be in resurrection even in your relationship with your wife. All the skills we acquire must be in resurrection.

Years ago, I often wrote a letter two or three times because after the first writing I felt that some phrases were too natural and were not in resurrection. Hence, I destroyed the letter and began again. After exercising like this to write a letter, I would still wait a day before mailing it. My purpose in doing so was to determine whether or not that letter was truly in resurrection. We all must learn to do things and to have our being in resurrection. This is a basic matter.

X. THE TRANSFERRED NAPHTALITE NEEDING TO BE FETCHED OUT OF TYRE AND TO COME TO KING SOLOMON IN JERUSALEM WHERE GOD'S BUILDING IS

Hiram was fetched out of Tyre and was brought to King Solomon in Jerusalem. This means that the transferred Naphtalite must be fetched out of Tyre and come to King

Solomon in Jerusalem where God's building is (1 Kings 7:13-14). King Solomon was a type of Christ, and Jerusalem, the place where God's building was, signifies the church. Today's Solomon and God's present building are both in the church. In a very good sense, the church today is Jerusalem. Although your "Tyrian" father has died, your widowed "Danite" mother continues to exist, and you are in resurrection, you still need to come to the church because this is where God's building is. God will not build His temple in Tyre. Although you may be very useful, if you remain in Tyre, you will be useless as far as God's building is concerned. If you remain in Tyre, you may be qualified, but your standing, your ground, will be wrong. The Lord must fetch you out of Tyre and bring you to Jerusalem. If your "Tyrian" father dies, your "Danite" mother goes on living as a widow, and you are in resurrection and have come to Jerusalem, then you will be useful for God's building.

XI. THE CASES OF MOSES WITH JOSHUA AND PAUL WITH TIMOTHY

You are probably familiar with the cases of Moses with Joshua (Num. 27:15-23) and of Paul with Timothy (1 Tim. 1:1-3; 2 Tim. 1:1-2, 6-8; 2:1-3). Moses and Paul firstly became pillars themselves and later became pillar builders. Moses built Joshua and Paul built Timothy. Moses did not actually bring the children of Israel into the rest; Joshua, who was a pillar built up by Moses, did this. Likewise, Paul built up Timothy, and Timothy became a pillar standing to bear the church testimony. In the cases of both Moses and Paul we see that their "Tyrian" fathers died. In Philippians 3, Paul, speaking of his religious background, said, "What things were gain to me, those I counted loss for Christ." Paul had learned a great deal at the feet of Gamaliel (Acts 22:3), but Gamaliel, the source of Paul's skill, had to be cut off. However, Paul's human existence remained. Furthermore, both Moses and Paul were in resurrection. They were also fetched out of "Tyre" and brought to the place where God's building was. With Moses this building was the tabernacle, and with Paul it was the church. History records that Moses and Paul were more than useful in the hands of God. They were not only pillars; they were also pillar builders. This is the need in the church today. In order for this need to be met, we all must pray to the Lord, saying, "Lord, for the sake of Your building, make me a pillar and a pillar builder."

LIFE-STUDY OF GENESIS

MESSAGE EIGHTY-SEVEN

BEING TRANSFORMED

(8)

We have seen that Jacob twice set up a pillar in Bethel (28:18, 22; 35:14). Not only did he set up a pillar, but he called it "the house of God." As we have pointed out again and again, nearly every item in the book of Genesis is a seed of a truth developed in the following books of the Bible. Knowing this principle is basic to our understanding of the book of Genesis. If we would understand this book, we must follow the development of the items it contains throughout the following books of the Bible until they reach their ultimate consummation in the book of Revelation. In past messages we have considered the development of the pillar in 1 Kings, 2 Chronicles, and Jeremiah. Now we shall trace this development into the New Testament, where we have a clear word regarding three aspects of pillars: the apostles as pillars of the church, the church as a whole being the pillar, and the overcomers as pillars in the New Jerusalem.

(c) Related to the Building
of the Church

aa. The Apostles Being the Pillars
of the Church

Galatians 2:9 says that James, Cephas, and John were reputed to be pillars. Here Peter is called Cephas. We know that Cephas was Peter and that Peter was Cephas. In using the name Cephas in this verse, the Bible reminds us of the change of Peter's name. When Peter was first brought to the Lord, He changed his name from Simon to Cephas, which means a stone (John 1:42). Undoubtedly, this change of name indicated that the Lord's intention was to transform him into a stone for God's building. Although we are accustomed to reading of Peter and John, in Galatians 2:9 Paul purposely speaks of Cephas and John to show us that, if we would become pillars, we need to be transformed. The natural Simon must be transformed into a Cephas, a stone.

Now we must consider the question of how a natural man can become a pillar of the church. This can only be accomplished through transformation. According to the New Testament, transformation depends upon regeneration. By regeneration a new life is put into us. This life is a life that will transform us. By our natural birth we inherited an old, sinful, natural life. This life is absolutely useless in making us pillars. But thank the Lord that regeneration imparts into us a life different from our natural life. This new life is the divine life, the very life of God. In the Gospel of John this life is called eternal life (John 3:16). The eternal life sown into us at the time of our regeneration is the seed of transformation. Hallelujah, all the regenerated ones have received this divine life! We all have this seed of transformation. However, although many Christians devote a great deal of attention to regeneration, very few pay attention to transformation. Few Christians have ever heard a message about transformation, and there may even be some among us who have never prayed for their own transformation. I strongly urge you to pray for your transformation. Formerly, we needed regeneration; now we need transformation.

A human being is composed of three parts: spirit, soul, and body (1 Thes. 5:23). When we believed in the Lord Jesus, called on His name, applied His blood, and received Him as our Redeemer and our life, the divine Spirit entered into our spirit as the Spirit of life. As a result, we were regenerated and received the divine life, which was sown into the depths of our being as the seed of transformation. But what about our soul, which is composed of the mind, the will, and the emotion? We have the divine life in our spirit, but we still need to be transformed in our mind. Romans 12:2 proves this: "Be transformed by the renewing of the mind." Transformation takes place through the renewing of our mind, emotion, and will. These basic inner parts of our being need transformation. This transformation will make us stones for God's building.

Through regeneration plus transformation we become stones for God's building. Today, God's building is the church, God's house, God's temple. First Peter 2:4 and 5 reveal that Christ is the living stone and that, when we, the regenerated ones, come to Him, we also become living stones to be built up into a spiritual house, which is the church as the temple of God. Today God's building is the church, but in the future it will be the New Jerusalem. If we read Revelation 21 carefully, we shall see that the New Jerusalem will be the enlargement of the temple of God. Today, the temple of God is a house, but in eternity the temple of God will be a city, which of course is much greater than a house. The New Jerusalem will be built with precious stones (Rev. 21:18-20); in it there will be no dust, clay, or wood. Our destiny is to be precious stones built into the New Jerusalem.

Now we come to the crucial matter of how clay can be transformed into stone. We were made clay (2:7; Rom. 9:21, 23), but the New Testament reveals that we are stones. There seems to be a contradiction here. From the natural perspective we are clay, but from the spiritual, transformed perspective we are stones. But how does this transformation from clay to stone take place? Transformation is the adding of Christ into our being. To be transformed is not only to have Christ imparted into our spirit; it is to have Him spread from our spirit into every inward part of our being. Very few Christians have seen this.

Recently, I was told of a group of Christians who argue strongly that Christ is only in the third heaven and that He is not in us. The Bible reveals and we also preach that Christ today is in the third heaven at the right hand of God. Nevertheless, He is also in us. Both matters are covered in Romans 8. Romans 8:34 says that Christ is at the right hand of God interceding for us, and Romans 8:10 says that Christ is in us. Hence, Christ is both in heaven and in us. But these Christians ask, "Was not Christ resurrected with a body of flesh and bones? Since Christ has been resurrected with a body of flesh and bones, how could He get into you?" According to the

Bible, we definitely believe that Christ was resurrected physically with a body of flesh and bones (Luke 24:39). But listen to this: On the day of resurrection the resurrected Christ, having a body of flesh and bones, came into a locked room (John 20:19-20). How did He get into the room? He certainly did not appear as a ghost (Luke 24:37, 39). We must reverently confess that we cannot figure out this matter.

Colossians 1:27 says, "Christ in you, the hope of glory." Although Christ was resurrected with a body of flesh and bones, He became the life-giving Spirit in resurrection (1 Cor. 15:45). As the life-giving Spirit, Christ is in our spirit (2 Tim. 4:22). Furthermore, Christ is growing and increasing within us. The more Christ is added into us, the more we are transformed from clay into stone. I doubt that those who refuse to admit that Christ is in them are able to be transformed. They surely could not deliver a message on transformation. But we are not simply concerned for messages—we are concerned for transformation. We need to be transformed, and transformation is only possible by having Christ imparted into us each day. Morning after morning, we need to gain more of Christ. Each day Christ must be increasingly added into our being.

Consider the example of Peter, a Galilean fisherman. Peter was rough, uncultured, and of a quick disposition. He was quick to talk, quick to act, and quick to make mistakes. Peter also had the good point of being quick to repent, to return. The Peter in the Gospels was eventually changed into another person called Cephas in the Epistles. We may take, as an illustration of this, Peter's slow response to the vision in Acts 10:9-16. There is a marked difference between the slow Peter in Acts 10 and the quick Peter in the Gospels. Furthermore, Peter's two epistles reveal that he had become a cautious person. By this we see that his disposition had been changed and that his being had been transformed. He had absolutely become another person. His word concerning Paul (2 Pet. 3:15-16) proves that he had been transformed and had become another person.

Recall that one day Paul rebuked Peter to his face (Gal. 2:11). If we put Galatians 2 together with 2 Peter 3 we see that the Peter who had been rebuked by Paul spoke kind words concerning Paul and positive words concerning his writings. In most situations today, if one brother rebuked another, the brother who received the rebuke would not forgive the brother who rebuked him. Because this is the practice, one brother rarely rebukes another. In today's Christianity we seldom hear of rebukes, but of political talk. Some may praise others to their face, but criticize them behind their back. This is the political practice of today's Christianity. Most Christians are politicians. Paul, on the contrary, was not a politician; he was a frank, direct, and straight rebuker. He even rebuked Peter. According to our concept, Peter should have said, "Who are you? When I was the leading apostle, you were still a young man persecuting the church. Now, as a newcomer, you have neither the qualifications nor the position to rebuke me." Peter, however, did not react in this manner. In his word in 2 Peter 3 he acknowledged that he was inferior to Paul in writing of God's economy. He admitted that some things Paul said were deep and difficult to understand. This attitude indicates that Peter was no longer natural, but that he had been transformed into another person. I hope that after a number of years many of you will be so transformed that you will be honest, frank, and straight in rebuking others, and that those who are rebuked will be transformed to receive such a rebuke. By reading the New Testament we clearly see that Peter was transformed into Cephas, one of the pillars of the church. Peter, who himself was a living stone, said that we also are living stones. This means that in order to be pillars we must be transformed by having Christ added into us.

bb. The Church Being the Pillar of the Truth

In the New Testament we are also told that the whole church is the pillar. First Timothy 3:15 says, "But if I delay, that you may know how one ought to conduct himself in the house of God, which is the church of the living God, the pillar and base of the truth." It is difficult to understand the word truth in this verse. Some say that truth means doctrine. Although this is correct, it is inadequate. In Greek, the word truth denotes something real and solid. Hence, truth means reality. However, truth is not simply a solid reality, but also the expression of this reality. Truth is not vain doctrine; it is the expression of reality, doctrine constituted with reality and conveying that reality. The church is the pillar bearing the truth, that is, bearing the expression of the reality.

The reality borne by the church is revealed in 1 Timothy 3:16: "And confessedly, great is the mystery of godliness, who was manifested in the flesh, vindicated in the Spirit, seen by angels, preached among the nations, believed on in the world, taken up in glory." The truth in verse 15, the expression of the reality, is the mystery of godliness in verse 16. The mystery of godliness is God manifested in the flesh. When Christ was on earth, He was God manifested in the flesh. Outwardly, He was a man in the flesh; inwardly, in actuality and in reality, He was God. God in His reality was manifested in the man Jesus. God was reality, and Jesus as a man in the flesh was the manifestation of God. This is the very truth mentioned in verse 15, and this is the mystery of godliness. Godliness means God-likeness. The mystery of godliness is the mystery of God-likeness. When Jesus lived on earth as a man in the flesh, the people who beheld Him saw in Him the likeness of God. Although He was a man, He expressed God. This God-likeness was a mystery. The mystery of godliness must be continued in the church today.

The church is the continuation of the mystery of godliness. In message eighty-six we saw that Christians have a mysterious part in their being. In principle, the whole church should be a mystery. If some unbelievers come into our meetings and survey the situation, they will not be able to understand it. Although we consider ourselves common and simple, the unbelievers will say, "What is this? What attracts them to these meetings? There is no entertainment or outstanding speaker. Who are these people? They seem to be neither modern nor old-fashioned. We cannot say what kind of people they are." The reason for this is that we are mysterious. Do not think that I am referring to our outward appearance. I am referring to something of God manifested in us. Because this is real yet invisible, it is difficult to define. If the church is merely pure, clean, gentle, humble, and holy, we have missed the mark. The church must be the continuation of the manifestation of God in the flesh. To some of our critics, the continuation of the manifestation of God in the church is a form of evolution into God. To accuse us of teaching evolution is a slander to us and a blasphemy to the Lord. The proper church life is a continuation of the manifestation of God in the flesh. This manifestation is the truth held by the church as the pillar. If as the church we hold this testimony, we shall be able to say that we are the continuation of the mystery of godliness.

We do not want to express our own holiness or anything of ourselves. We want only to express our God and to see Him manifested in our flesh. We admit that we are still flesh, but the very God who lives in our spirit will be manifested, expressed, in our flesh. This manifestation must not merely be individual, but corporate. The proper church life is the corporate manifestation of God in the flesh.

The only way the church can be the corporate expression of God in the flesh is by transformation. Everyone in the church must be transformed. Occasionally we refer to the older brothers or to the younger brothers. However, in the church we should not think of some as older ones and of others as younger, for we all are being transformed. Although we may not yet be fully transformed, we are at least in the process of transformation. Forget your age and concentrate upon the fact that you are in the process of transformation. If I still think of myself as a Chinese, I am finished. In the church there is neither old nor young, Chinese nor American, Jew nor Greek (Col. 3:11). In the church we are being changed by having Christ added into us. You should not be an old brother or a young brother, but a brother into whom Christ is being added daily. The older ones may need to remind the younger ones not to call them older brothers, and the younger ones may need to ask the older ones not to speak of them as young brothers. Furthermore, we should not refer to some brothers as "Yankees" and to others as Southerners. There are neither "Yankees" nor Southerners in the church; there are only transformed brothers. There is no black, white, yellow, red, Jew, or Greek; instead, there are only the transformed people—people into whom Christ is being added daily and who are the expression of God in Christ. This is the church as the pillar supporting and bearing the mystery of godliness.

After hearing the messages on Hiram, the builder of the pillars, many young people have been motivated to further their education. This is excellent. In order to be a capable pillar builder you need to acquire a good education and to experience the termination of the source of that education. However, if you earn the highest degree but are lacking Christ, you are still nothing. The basic element that can constitute you into a pillar is not a college degree; it is Christ added into you. No matter how many degrees you have, if you are short of Christ, you cannot be a pillar. The basic element in being a pillar is neither your education nor capability, but your Christ, the very Christ added into your being. This is the essential factor in being constituted as a pillar. A pillar must be the continuation of the manifestation of God in the flesh.

(d) Consummated in the New Jerusalem

Now we must go on to the pillars in the New Jerusalem. Revelation 3:12 says, "He who overcomes, I will make him a pillar in the temple of My God, and he shall by no means go out anymore, and I will write upon him the name of My God and the name of the city of My God, the New Jerusalem, which descends out of heaven from My God, and My new name." In this verse we see the consummation of the pillar in the New Jerusalem.

aa. The Overcomer Who Keeps the Lord's Word and Denies Not His Name Being Made a Pillar in God's Enlarged Temple

According to Revelation 3:12, we all may become pillars in the New Jerusalem. In Revelation 3:8 the Lord Jesus said, "You have a little power and have kept My word and have not denied My name." Then in Revelation 3:11 He said, "Hold fast what you have that no one take your crown." Firstly, the Lord tells those in the church in Philadelphia that they have a little power, that they have kept His word, and that they have not denied His name. Then He tells them to hold fast what they have. They must keep the word of the Lord and not deny the name of the Lord. If we do this, we shall be overcomers, and the Lord will write upon us the name of His God, the name of the New Jerusalem, and His new name. Now we must consider what it means to keep the word of the Lord and not to deny the name of the Lord. These matters are deep and difficult to explain.

A superficial understanding of keeping the Lord's word is that the Lord speaks a certain word and we keep it; He tells us to do something and we do it. This is correct, but it is shallow. In order to keep the Lord's word we must do two things: on the positive side we need to receive all that He is into us, and, on the negative side, we need to kill all our concepts and opinions. It is not simply a matter of the Lord telling us to love one another or to wash one another's feet and of our proceeding to love others and to wash their feet. This understanding is too superficial. The Lord's word represents the Lord Himself. If we would receive the word as the expression of the Lord Himself, we must drop our opinions and concepts.

Your opinions frustrate you from keeping the Lord's word. Probably, you have rarely kept the word of the Lord because you have been hindered by your opinions. In this message we have been speaking about transformation. As Romans 12:2 indicates, transformation primarily deals with the mind. We are transformed by the renewing of the mind, which is the source of our concepts and opinions. To be transformed is to have our concepts and opinions slain. None of us can say that he has no opinions or concepts. Some may ask, "Should we be wooden boards without any feeling, knowledge, or sense?" Of course not. We need to be living. But the more living we are, the more we are filled with opinions and concepts. The more I have prayed about this matter and considered my experience, the more I have realized that to keep the word of the Lord is actually to be transformed.

The way to be transformed is to receive the word of the Lord into us and to keep it. Most of us do not keep the Lord's word because we are hindered by our opinions and our concepts. Everyone is opinionated. Those who minister the Word often pray that the Lord would remove the opinions of those hearing the Word and take away the veils of their concepts. A word may be clearly uttered, but your concepts and opinions may frustrate you from keeping it. If we would keep the Lord's word, we must firstly drop our opinions and then have the Lord Jesus added into our being.

Now let us consider what it means not to deny the Lord's name. A name always denotes a person. When I call a brother's name, the brother himself comes. Therefore, not to deny the name of the Lord means not to deny the Person of the Lord.

All denominational names, such as Baptist, Methodist, Lutheran, and Presbyterian, must be forsaken. A name means a great deal. Although you may not realize it, if you take a denominational designation, you are actually rejecting the name of Christ, and thus you are rejecting the Person of Christ. Although you may not intend to do this, this is nonetheless the fact. If it is not your intention to deny the name of Christ, then you should not have any denominational name. In the past some missionaries and pastors have consulted me about this matter. They have all told me that they do not care for the denominational names. I told them that, since they did not care for these names, they should forsake them. It is a serious matter to take another name above the Lord's name. Apparently, for many, it is insufficient merely to be a Christian. They take on other names and say, "I am a Lutheran," "I am a Presbyterian," or, "I am a Baptist." To do this is to deny the Lord's name. One hundred and fifty years ago the Brethren saw the light on this matter and forsook every other name and declared that they held just one name—the name of the Lord Jesus Christ. This is the unique name. However, it is not merely a name in letters, but a name in Person.

If we do not deny the name of the Lord, then we have His Person as ours, and His Person becomes our designation. When you go to work, perhaps in a large corporation with hundreds of employees, there is no need for you to label yourself as a Christian. You simply need to express the Person of Christ. To fail to express the Person of Christ actually means to deny His name. We must live in such a way that Christ is expressed through us. If we express Christ, the One we express will, in the words of others, become our designation. Others will say that we are Christians. The Person we express becomes our name, our designation. People will not say that you are Chinese or a "Yankee." The only designation they will give you is that of being a Christian.

Approximately forty years ago, a brother was an employee in a large company. His fellow workers called him "Jesus." When they saw him, they said, "This is Jesus," apparently in a despising way. At the time of the Japanese invasion of China, many of the employees in this company were planning to escape. Having money and other valuables that had to be left behind, they looked for someone to whom they could entrust their possessions. After considering a number of possibilities, they finally decided to entrust their money and belongings to the brother, the one they called "Jesus." This shows that they were trusting in Jesus. The brother, of course, never said that his name was Jesus. Rather, he expressed the Person of Christ in his living, and his life was his designation. This is the true significance of not denying the name of the Lord. The church in Philadelphia lived by the Lord, and His life was lived out by that church. Therefore, His Person became the name of those saints.

To keep the word of the Lord and not to deny the name of the Lord means to forsake our opinions and concepts, to receive the Lord's word into us, and to gain more and more of the Lord Himself. If we do this, we shall live Him out as a Person. The name of this Person is Jesus. To keep the Lord's word is not merely a doctrinal matter, and to confess His name is not simply to utter a few statements. To keep His word means to receive Him into our being, letting go of our concepts and opinions that He may have the ground within us; and not to deny His name is to live out Christ as a Person so that He becomes our designation. This indicates transformation.

bb. Bearing the Name of Christ's God, the Name of the City of Christ's God, and Christ's New Name

In Revelation 3:12 the Lord said that He would write upon the overcomer "the name of My God and the name of the city of My God, the New Jerusalem, which descends out of heaven from My God, and My new name." In Revelation Christ called God, "My God" because in this book He stands on the position of a sent One, as One sent by God to accomplish His economy. The Lord also held to this position in the four Gospels, always standing on the ground of One who had been sent by God. He had been sent by God and from with God to accomplish God's purpose. He never acted according to His own will, but always according to God's will (John 6:38). Even when He was on the cross, He said, "My God, My God, why have You forsaken Me?" (Matt. 27:46). We also must stand on this position today, saying, "I am a sent one. I have been sent by the Lord to accomplish His purpose. I have no other position, opinion, or concept. It is His will, not my will, that must be done." To say, "My God," indicates that we do not act on our own; it indicates that we are doing the will of God. We are not working for our career; we are accomplishing His purpose. Having the name "My God" written upon you designates you as this kind of person. You, like the Lord Jesus when He was on earth, are not doing your own will, but are accomplishing God's will. You do not act on your own, but constantly walk in God's will. This is the significance of the name of "My God."

The Lord also promised to write upon the overcomer the name of the New Jerusalem, the city of His God. This is deep. It means that the New Jerusalem is a building, not according to any man's will, but according to the will of God. All those built into this city are people like the Jesus revealed in the four Gospels. They do not act according to their own will, but according to God's will. Only those who are like this are qualified to be labeled with the name of the city of Christ's God, the New Jerusalem.

Finally, in Revelation 3:12 the Lord promised to write upon the overcomer His new name. If we are the kind of person described in this message, we shall surely have new experiences of Christ. Most Christians have only the limited experience of Christ as their Redeemer. Not many have the experience of Christ as their life. Most of those who do experience Christ as life experience this in a shallow way. How long is your experience of Christ? Your experience of Him should not be a mere fraction of an inch; it must be many miles in length. Christ is not only our Redeemer and our life—He is our King, Prophet, Priest, light, power, righteousness, holiness, transformation, and many other things. Some hymns in our hymnal list more than fifty items of what Christ is to us. The more you experience Christ, the newer He will be to you, and the more His name will be written upon you. Firstly, Christ as Redeemer is written upon you. Later, Christ as life, light, humility, patience, and love will also be written upon you. His name is inexhaustible. The writing of His name upon you depends upon your experience. The more you experience Him, the longer will be the writing of this name. This is like a movie camera that operates as long as the automobile in which the photographer sits is moving. When the automobile stops, the camera stops as well. No one can say what is the new name of Christ spoken of in this verse because it is simply the designation of your new experience of Christ. When you experience Christ in a certain way, that aspect of Christ will become your designation, the new name written upon you. If we would become pillars, we need to be transformed by having Christ added into us again and again. In this way our experience of Christ will be lengthened, and we shall say, "Not my will, but His will"; we shall not act on our own, but according to His heart's desire. Then the name of God, the name of the city of God, and the Lord's new name will be written upon us.

LIFE-STUDY OF GENESIS

MESSAGE EIGHTY-EIGHT

THE WAY TO BE PERFECTED AS A PILLAR

In this message we need to consider how we can be perfected as pillars for the Lord's move. The kind of pillar I am talking about, of course, is the pillar in Solomon's temple (1 Kings 7:13-22), the pillar in Bethel (Gen. 28:18, 22; 35:14).

OUR NEED TO BE IN TODAY'S BETHEL

If we mean business with the Lord to become pillars, then we must discover where Bethel is today. Otherwise, we shall be seeking the right thing in the wrong place. If we remain in the Catholic Church, the denominations, the charismatic movement, or the free groups, it will be impossible for us to be perfected as pillars. Do not think that such a statement indicates we are being narrow-minded or shortsighted. We must be in today's Bethel, the church. There is no other place for us to be made pillars in God's building. The pillars perfected in other places are not pillars for Bethel, God's building, but for other things. Through the past centuries, some spiritual giants have been perfected to be pillars for the denominations, for the mission fields, or for certain movements. However, through my years of observation, I have not seen any pillars perfected for the Lord's building outside the local churches. We must be clear that the pillars about which we are speaking are the genuine pillars for God's building. If we want to be such a pillar, then we must ask where God's building, today's Bethel, is. We should not take this matter lightly.

A PERSONAL TESTIMONY

In 1933 I was burdened by the Lord, even forced by Him, to give up my job and to serve Him full-time. I had not studied in a Bible school or seminary. At the time I was working in a corporation. When the Lord was dealing with me about giving up my job, I could not eat or sleep well for three weeks. To serve the Lord full-time required an extreme exercise of my faith, and nothing in my environment favored this decision. I simply did not know how I would care for my living. Eventually, however, I had no choice except to quit my job. After I made this decision, I received a brief note from Brother Nee. In this note Brother Nee said, "Brother Witness, as to your future, I feel that you have to serve the Lord with your full time. How do you feel about it? May the Lord lead you." This note, dated August 17, 1933, the middle of my three-week struggle with the Lord, was a strong confirmation. I had resigned from the corporation, but I had little faith; I was still doubting that I had made the right decision. At that very juncture, that note arrived from Brother Nee. After I read it, I said, "The Lord willing, I will visit this brother and find out why he wrote that note to me at that time."

With this purpose in mind, I went to Shanghai to visit Brother Nee, and he received me as his guest. I stayed with him for several months and I received great help from him. Of course, my first question was why he had written that note on August 17. He told me that as his boat was sailing back to China on the Mediterranean Sea and he was sitting silently in his cabin alone, he was burdened to pray for the Lord's move in China. While he was praying, the Lord pointed out to him that he had to write me that note. Then I told him that the date on which he wrote this note was in the middle of my three-week struggle with the Lord. This report confirmed for Brother Nee that what he had written was absolutely right. Through this note he and I were builded together even more than before. We were deeply assured that the Lord had put us together. From this time, he treated me as a new learner, and I honored and respected him, my senior co-worker, as one who could perfect me.

Because there was not that much work for Brother Nee and me to do in the early days, I often went to him in his home for long periods of time. At these times he perfected me in many different ways. Before the Lord I can testify that we never spent any time in gossip. Brother Nee, an outstanding gift given by the Lord to perfect others, always used the time to perfect me. He certainly knew what I needed. He gave me the proper understanding of church history from the first century until the present; he shared with me the biographies of nearly all the founders of the different denominations; and he perfected me with respect to the inner life, the church life, and the Lord's move.

ONE FLOW

One day Brother Nee told me that he and the other co-workers were burdened that I move to Shanghai with my family to stay with them and work with them. He asked me to bring this matter to the Lord. As I took the matter to the Lord and prayed about it, the Lord showed me from the book of Acts that in His move on earth there is only one flow. This flow started from Jerusalem and spread to Antioch, and from Antioch it turned to Europe. The Lord told me that for His move in China there should not be two flows or two origins. I had been burdened for north China. Before I had gone to see Brother Nee, I had conducted a thorough study on the Song of Songs in the summer of 1933. But although I was definitely burdened for north China, Brother Nee and the co-workers felt that I should move to Shanghai, stay there, and work with them. At this time the Lord showed me that I had to get into the one flow that had started from Shanghai. I saw that from Shanghai the flow would proceed to the north and to other parts of the country. Therefore, I decided to move to Shanghai and to stay there. From that time onward, I have been in the flow. I have been absolutely clear that this is the Lord's flow and His move on earth in His recovery. Using today's word, I knew that I had found Bethel.

THE MINISTRY RESPONSIBLE FOR THE FLOW

Because I knew I was in the Lord's flow and that this flow had already started, I also realized that there was a ministry responsible for that flow. As the result of seeing this, I strongly decided to forget all my past learning and experience. The fact that I had been able to conduct a detailed study on Song of Songs indicates that I had some knowledge and that I could do something. I had learned a good deal about the Bible in my seven and a half years with the Brethren. I knew the types, the prophecies, and various other things. Moreover, a church had been established through me. Nevertheless, I realized that the Lord's flow on the earth must be one, that the flow had already begun, and that there was a ministry carrying on this flow. I knew that I had to be in the flow and to be under the ministry responsible for the flow.

Those who were with us in the early years can testify that, apart from the messages I gave in the meetings, I never said anything. In view of the fact that Brother Nee was present, I dropped all my concepts, all my learnings, and all my experiences. He was the one used by the Lord to start the flow and he had the ministry to carry on the flow. There was no need for my opinion. However, this does not mean that I did nothing. During the next eighteen or twenty years, I did a great deal. But everything was according to Brother Nee's leading, not according to my opinion. I never ministered anything according to myself; I only ministered the messages delivered by Brother Nee. In those years I never expressed my opinion or concept; instead, I wholly followed Brother Nee.

The Lord is flowing in His move on earth. This flow was not started by you, but by others. Furthermore, there is a ministry responsible for the flow. It is difficult for me to speak about this because now the matter is very much related to me. If I were still on the mainland and the flow were related to Brother Nee's ministry, I would have the ground to say much more.

THE SECRET TO BEING PERFECTED
TO BE A PILLAR

Let me now tell you the secret to being solidly perfected to be a strong pillar for the Lord's move. Certain brothers have been perfected because they have had no concepts of their own. Recently, one brother declared strongly that he only knows to follow the ministry of Brother Lee and to absorb everything of this ministry. There have been others among us who were quite opinionated. They often said, "Brother Lee says such-and-such. Is this right? Is the church right? Just a week ago, I learned about a mistake made by the church." None of these opinionated ones has yet been perfected. But those who have been perfected to be pillars are not like this. Even when they see certain mistakes, they forget about them, having no time to waste discussing them. They only desire to soak in all the positive things.

FEASTING ON THE POSITIVE THINGS

According to God's principle in His creation, in order for anything to grow there is the need for a negative side. Take the example of a chicken. We all appreciate chicken eggs, breasts, and legs, but we certainly do not care for chicken dung, feathers, and bones. Nevertheless, without dung, feathers, and bones, a chicken cannot grow. In order for a chicken to be a chicken, it must have these things. But it is not our portion to eat them. We should enjoy the eggs, the breasts, and the legs, and forget the dung, the feathers, and the bones. If we concentrate on the positive aspects of the chicken, we shall receive much nourishment.

I admit that the church in Los Angeles has made certain mistakes, and I confess that I have made mistakes. The elders can testify of this. Everybody makes mistakes. No one can deny this. I have had to make mistakes in order to grow. These mistakes are my "dung." If you eat this, you are foolish. I also admit that I have "feathers." The church in Los Angeles also has had a certain amount of "feathers" and "bones." However, without these "feathers," "bones," and "dung," neither the church in Los Angeles nor my ministry would be able to exist. Do you intend to gather up the "feathers" and say, "Look! This is the church in Los Angeles. Look! This is what Brother Lee has done. See all these awful 'feathers.'" If you do this, you will not damage the church in Los Angeles or my ministry, but you will surely damage yourself. To do this is not wise. These who have been perfected to be pillars, who surely are not less intelligent than you, are wise. Their eyes are much clearer than yours. But they refuse to devote their attention to the negative things. They would say, "Although Brother Lee has some 'dung,' he has a great many eggs. I don't care for the 'dung' issuing out of his ministry—I want to eat all the 'eggs,' 'breasts,' and 'legs.' I have no time to hear about 'feathers' and 'bones.'" Let us follow the example of such brothers to forget the negative things and to feast upon the "eggs," "breasts," and "legs." This is my burden in this message.

Are you in Anaheim as a spy, investigating whether or not Witness Lee has any "dung"? I cannot live without "dung." To be sure, both "feathers" and "bones" can be found here in Anaheim. The elders have made many "bones." But I would stand, even dance, upon all the "bones" they have made; I would not be so foolish as to eat them.

Three or four of us knew Brother Nee very intimately. He fully opened himself to us, and we knew his imperfections. But we realized that these imperfections were the "dung" that enabled him to exist. Unlike others, we would not cling to his "feathers," nor to the "bones" of the "chicken" in Shanghai. If we had done this, we would have sacrificed ourselves. I never suffered such self-inflicted damage. Rather, I enjoyed the fresh, nourishing "eggs," "breasts," and "legs" of Brother Nee's ministry. When a great turmoil was aroused against his ministry, I was not ashamed to say that I was an absolute follower of Brother Nee. I did not care what others said about his mistakes. I only knew how grateful I was to him for the perfection he had rendered to me. I knew the nourishment I had received from him. Even when we are in the New Jerusalem, I shall be able to say that the Lord used Brother Nee to perfect me. Apart from his ministry, I would never be the person I am today.

How foolish it would be for anyone in the church to devote his time to finding "dung" or stuffing his pockets with "feathers," saying, "This is a 'feather' from that 'chicken' Witness Lee, and these are the 'bones' of the church in Anaheim. Don't you know that the church in Anaheim has made mistakes?" If this is your intention, you are wasting your time. You are in the wrong place. Neither Witness Lee nor the church in Anaheim would pay you for exposing them. But do not think that we are afraid of being exposed. Whatever Witness Lee is, he is what he is. Whether the church is genuine or not, the church is what the church is. Neither the church in Anaheim nor my ministry is afraid of exposure. On the contrary, we appreciate it. But what will you gain by exposing us?

FINDING THE FLOW AND GETTING INTO IT

The Lord is still working and moving to accomplish something on earth. In order for Him to fulfill His purpose there must be a flow. Among the many activities taking place in Christian circles, there must be the flow of the Lord's move. Surely you believe that the Lord is still living, moving, and working on earth. According to the principle, there must be one flow of the Lord on earth. The Bible reveals that there has always been just one flow. There was one flow with Abel, Noah, and Abraham, and at the end of the Old Testament there was still only one flow. It is the same in the New Testament. Because the Lord is still living, moving, and working on earth, there must also be just one flow on earth today.

Since there is only one flow on earth, we should do everything necessary to find out where the flow is. It is certainly worthwhile to travel and study in order to find it. I am not a stupid person who follows things blindly. Before I leaped into the flow, I searched and researched thoroughly. I had given up my job, my family, and everything I had. I did not want to waste my sacrifice. Hence, I took time to study the matter. Eventually, I was convinced that this is the flow, and for more than forty-five years I have not had a doubt about it.

After we have seen that there is one flow and we have discovered where the flow is, we must get into it, forgetting our past learnings, concepts, understandings, and viewpoints. As far as the flow is concerned, all this means nothing. For many, it is rather late to say that they know nothing. They should have said this at the very beginning. From the very day I told Brother Nee that I would move to Shanghai, work with them, and learn of the brothers, I abandoned everything and followed that unique ministry. I shall never regret that decision. Hallelujah for that choice! No one can measure the nourishment and perfection I received as the result of turning this way. Certain brothers among us have been the same. They have no time to care for "dung," "feathers," or "bones."

They only have time to absorb all that is in this flow. This is the proper way to be perfected as useful pillars for the Lord's move.

LIFE-STUDY OF GENESIS

MESSAGE EIGHTY-NINE

BEING TRANSFORMED

(9)

At Bethel Jacob did some very significant things. He built an altar, set up a pillar, poured a drink offering upon the pillar, and then poured oil upon the pillar (35:7, 14-15). In this message we shall consider Jacob's pouring the drink offering and the oil upon the pillar he had set up.

(2) Pouring a Drink Offering upon the Pillar

Remember that nearly every item mentioned in the book of Genesis is the seed of a truth developed in the following books of the Bible. Because 35:14 is the first mention of the drink offering, this verse is the seed of the drink offering. If we had only this verse, it would be difficult to know the meaning of the drink offering. In order to understand the significance of the drink offering, we must trace its development in both the Old Testament and in the New Testament.

We have pointed out that Jacob twice set up a pillar in Bethel. The first time he did not pour a drink offering upon the pillar; he simply poured oil upon it. The reason Jacob poured oil but not wine upon the pillar the first time was that in the Bible oil does not require very much experience on our part, but wine depends upon our experience. At the time of Jacob's first visit to Bethel, he did not have any experience of the Lord. Rather, he was a young supplanter and had no wine to pour out to the Lord. Thus, in chapter twenty-eight he could not pour out the drink offering. But twenty years later, after he had been touched by the Lord and had been somewhat transformed, he returned to Bethel. Because he had had some experience, he had wine to pour out upon the pillar as a drink offering to the Lord. Please keep in mind that the drink offering is absolutely related to our experience.

(a) In Addition to the Basic Offerings after the Experience of the Riches of Christ

Although all the offerings are types of Christ and are for our experience, there is a difference between the basic offerings and the drink offering. The sin offering, one of the basic offerings, was a type of Christ for the experience of sinners. Before sinners come to offer the sin offering, they do not have any experience. They gain experience by presenting the sin offering to God. No experience is required beforehand. Before you can pour out a drink offering, however, you must have a measure of experience. Without experience, you will not be able to have this offering because the drink offering is composed of our experience of Christ.

In the first seven chapters of Leviticus we have the five basic offerings: the burnt offering, the meal offering, the peace offering, the sin offering, and the trespass offering. There is no need to experience Christ before you offer Him as these basic offerings. But the drink offering is absolutely dependent upon our experience. This is quite important. Many believers have no understanding of the basic offerings, much less an understanding of the drink offering. The reason for this is that they are short of the real experiences of Christ. By the Lord's mercy we in His recovery must experience Christ in a practical, daily way. Daily we should experience Him as our burnt offering, meal offering, peace offering, sin offering, and trespass offering. In the beginning we offer Christ only in this way. But as we progress in our experience of Christ, we eventually discover an offering that is in addition to these basic offerings—the drink offering.

Suppose a certain man has been saved for just one day. He certainly has had no time to have the experience of Christ. But if he remains in the proper church life, the saints will help him to realize that he needs to live by Christ, taking Christ as his life in a practical way. As he learns to live by Christ, he will gradually realize that Christ is so much to him. The saints will no doubt help him to see that Christ is his burnt offering. He will realize that he should be absolutely for God; however, he will find that he is not able to be absolute. Nevertheless, Christ is his absoluteness. Through this experience, Christ will become his burnt offering for God's satisfaction. Furthermore, he will enjoy Christ as his meal offering, as the One who not only satisfies God, but who also feeds and supplies him. Then he will daily take Christ as his food, and Christ will nourish him and support him to live in the presence of God that God might be satisfied. In this way he will experience Christ as the meal offering. In like manner, he will experience the other basic offerings. By experiencing Christ in this way, he will eventually become a person filled and saturated with Christ. The very Christ who saturates him will be his wine, and the brother himself will be saturated with this wine and actually become one with the wine.

Some may wonder what ground we have for saying that Christ is wine. This is not my word; it is the Lord's word in Matthew 9:17. In this verse the Lord said, "Neither do they put new wine into old wineskins; otherwise, the wineskins burst, and the wine pours out, and the wineskins are destroyed; but they put new wine into fresh wineskins, and both are preserved." The Lord spoke this word in His answer to some disciples of John the Baptist who asked Him why His disciples did not fast (Matt. 9:14). The Lord wisely answered their question in a marvelous way with two parables. Firstly, He said, "No one puts a patch of unshrunk cloth on an old garment, for that which fills it up pulls away from the garment, and a worse tear is made" (Matt. 9:16). Secondly, He spoke about not putting new wine into old wineskins. What is this new cloth and new wine? Both the new cloth and the new wine are Christ. The new cloth is Christ as our new, unique, complete, and perfect righteousness for us to be justified before God. As the new cloth Christ is our righteousness to cover us. The new wine is Christ as the stirring life, as the life that stirs us up to make us happy and even "crazy." To be "crazy" is to be drunken. Christ as the new cloth covers us outwardly and Christ as the new wine stirs us and makes us "crazy" inwardly. In other words, Christ causes us to be drunken. All Christians must be "crazy" like this.

In the summer of 1935 Brother Nee stayed in my home town. During this time we had a conference in which we were all "crazy." Brother Nee did not stir us up to be "crazy"; we were "crazy" already. When he saw how "crazy" we were, he gave us a supplementary message telling us that we all need to be "crazy," beside ourselves (2 Cor. 5:13). He said that if any Christian has never been "crazy," then he is not yet up to standard. He said, "If you are always nice, formal, gentle, and regulated, you are below standard. You must be 'crazy' in the Lord like a drunkard."

Most Christians today are cold, quiet, and dead. The dead are formal and never make mistakes. The most regulated place on earth is a cemetery. Everyone there is quiet and orderly and never disturbs others. Most Christians are like this. Although they think this is beautiful, it is actually dreadful; it is a stench. Christians should be living. The reason many are not living is that they are short of the experiences of Christ. If we experience Christ day after day, eventually the Christ we experience will become wine in us. The more we experience Christ, the "crazier" we shall become. Since the time you were saved, how often have you been "crazy" in your fellowship with the Lord? Have you ever been in a state where you were so happy that you were not able to control yourself, even beside yourself with joy? Have you ever been so joyful that you did not know whether to jump, to dance, or to shout? The more we are "crazy" like this with the Lord, the better. Not only the young people, but even the older brothers and sisters should be "crazy" in their inner chamber with the Lord. As we are with the Lord, we must say, "Oh, what joy! What wine! I simply cannot stand it!" This is the experience of Christ as wine.

If we experience Christ as our sin offering time after time, this offering will eventually become wine. The reason is that Christ as the sin offering will make us happy and cause us to rejoice. However, if you very seldom enjoy Christ as your sin offering, it will not become wine in your experience. But if you experience Christ as the sin offering, and as the other basic offerings daily, Christ as all these offerings will become wine and cause you to be exceedingly happy and joyful. The more we experience Christ in all His riches, the more the elements of His riches will make us "crazy." Thus, whatever we experience of Christ will become our new wine.

In Matthew 9:16 and 17 the Lord told the disciples of John the Baptist that He came as the new cloth to cover us and as the new wine to satisfy us and to stir us up. How we need to experience Christ today! We need to experience Him as our burnt offering, meal offering, peace offering, sin offering, and trespass offering. Ultimately, our experience of Christ becomes the element within us stirring us up to be ecstatically happy. As we continue in this enjoyment, we shall even become one with the wine.

A drunkard is a man who has become one with the wine he drinks. Wine has saturated his whole being, and he even has the appearance and aroma of wine. We may say that this man is just wine. We Christians, like a drunkard saturated with wine, must be saturated with Christ until we become wine. Christ is the wine, but the wine must saturate us until it becomes us. When we become drunk of Christ and with Christ, we become wine to satisfy God, and we are qualified and ready to be a drink offering. The drink offering is not merely Christ Himself; it is the Christ who saturates us until Christ and we, we and Christ, become one.

In the first seven chapters of Leviticus, we have the basic offerings, but not the drink offering. The drink offering is mentioned in Leviticus 23:10-13, verses related to bringing the firstfruits of the harvest of the good land to the priest. Although the harvest was for the enjoyment of the children of Israel, they were required to bring the firstfruits of the harvest to God that He might have the first enjoyment. A sheaf of the firstfruits of the harvest was waved before the Lord. Hence, the firstfruits were a wave offering, typifying Christ in resurrection as the firstfruit being waved unto God (1 Cor. 15:20). Along with this sheaf of firstfruits, the children of Israel had to offer a burnt offering with a meal offering and a drink offering. It is in this context that the drink offering is mentioned in Leviticus.

There was no mention of the drink offering in connection with the five basic offerings in Leviticus 1 through 7 because at that time the offerers had no experience of Christ. They were like Jacob at Bethel the first time. But after they had entered into the good land, had experienced Christ, and had gained something to offer God, they were required to offer the drink offering to match their other offerings. Numbers 15:1-10 and 28:6-10 indicate that the drink offering always matched the basic offering. The drink offering was in proportion to the size of the basic offering: a fourth of a hin of wine for a lamb; a third of a hin for a ram; and half a hin for a bullock (Num. 15:4-10). This indicates that the more we experience Christ, the more of a drink offering we become. If you experience Christ only as a little lamb, you will be a drink offering of one fourth of a hin. But if you experience Him as a ram or as a bullock, you will become a larger drink offering. In other words, the more you offer Christ to God, the greater must be the drink offering to match it. Our experience proves that the more we experience Christ, the more we become the drink offering. As we offer Christ to God, spontaneously we have the drink offering to match our offering.

Although the lamb, the ram, and the bullock are types merely of Christ, the wine is not merely Christ. The Bible clearly indicates that the drink offering could not be offered to God by itself. It could only be presented to match one of the basic offerings. The basic offerings are Christ, but the drink offering is not just Christ Himself; it is the Christ who has saturated us until the wine has become us. Although the wine in Matthew 9:17 was only Christ, Paul said, "I am already being poured out as a drink offering" (2 Tim. 4:6, Gk.). The wine in 2 Timothy 4:6 was the Christ of Matthew 9:17 who had saturated Paul and who had made him wine. Formerly, this wine was only Christ; but now it becomes us that we may be poured out as a drink offering. This pouring out depends upon our experience of Christ. Here in Bethel, in God's house, we must be poured out as a drink offering.

Suppose a group of believers assembles every Sunday, but hardly any of them has the real experience of Christ. Could they be the drink offering? Certainly not. Because they cannot be a drink offering, this gathering of Christians cannot be considered as the house of God. The only pillar that can be rightly called the house of God is the pillar upon which the drink offering has been poured. If there is no drink offering poured upon the pillar, then there must be something wrong with that pillar. We must have doubts about any gathering of Christians in which there is no pouring out of the drink offering. In any meeting that is truly the house of God those meeting together will be a drink offering.

By the New Testament alone we cannot clearly and adequately understand spiritual things, especially the things concerning Christ and the church life. We also need the pictures in the Old Testament. We have a very vivid picture in Genesis 35. Here we see Jacob setting up a pillar and pouring the drink offering upon it. In chapter twenty-eight Jacob even called this pillar the house of God. There must have been a reason for all this to be recorded in the Bible. The reason is that the pillar indicates that the house of God is a matter of the building. If we do not have the drink offering poured out upon the pillar, it is questionable that we have the genuine building. Although many are talking about the building—thank the Lord for this—we must still ask whether or not a drink offering has been poured out upon the pillar.

The drink offering does not come from wine out of the winepress; it comes from our experience of drinking the wine. The winepress itself cannot produce a drink offering. God will not be satisfied merely with wine from the winepress. He will be fully satisfied with those who have enjoyed Christ as wine to such an extent that they have become drunk with Christ and have themselves become the wine to satisfy God. This wine is not the direct wine from the winepress; it is the indirect wine from those who drink Christ as the wine. This is deep. I believe that if many among us continue to go on with the Lord for another period of time, they will become such a drink offering and will be able to say, "Lord Jesus, I am already being poured out upon You as a drink offering." No recently saved person can say this. But there are some among us who can faithfully and honestly say with full assurance that they are already being poured out as a drink offering for the Lord. Wherever there is the drink offering, there is also the pillar set up as the house of God. This matter is deep, practical, and touches something deep in our experience. It touches us very deeply to see a person who is so saturated with Christ that his only interest is Christ and the church.

(b) For the Priestly Service

In Exodus 29 is the consecration of the priesthood. In verses 38 through 42 we are told that the priests had to offer the daily continual burnt offering with the drink offering. This indicates that in the priestly service the drink offering is needed to match the continual burnt offering.

(c) For the Nazarite

The drink offering was also related to the law of the Nazarite (Num. 6:13-17). A Nazarite was a person wholly consecrated to God. When the days of a Nazarite's separation were fulfilled, he had to offer a burnt offering, a sin offering, and a peace offering. Along with these offerings, he also had to offer a drink offering. The Nazarite was qualified to offer the drink offering because he was one who had experienced God to a great degree. This also proves that the drink offering comes from our experiences of the Lord. If we do not experience Him, we cannot have a drink offering. The drink offering is not merely the Lord Himself objectively; it is our subjective experience of being made one with the Lord to the extent that He becomes us. The Christ whom we experience in this subjective way is the wine we pour out to satisfy God for God's building.

(d) For the Church Life

We have pointed out that a drunkard's only interest is wine. His mind is constantly preoccupied with thoughts of wine. Even his dreams are dreams of wine. We must be like this about the church, the house of God. Besides Bethel, we should have no other interest. Consider the example of the Apostle Paul. His writings reveal that he was "crazy" for the church; he was drunk with Christ and interested only in God's house, God's temple. His terms for Bethel were "the church" and "the Body." He was drunk for the church. Some have said, "You church people are crazy. The only thing you know is the church." Once a lady approached me after a meeting and said, "Mr. Lee, why do you always talk about the church? Why don't you speak about the family life?" I answered, "I don't talk about the family because you talk about it so much. I must be interested in the church." The church should be our only interest. What is your interest today—school? business? family? My only interest is the church. We all need to be such "drunkards" for the church. Before his martyrdom, Paul said, "I am already being poured out as a drink offering." If our only interest is the church, then we are ready to say the same thing. It has only been through experience that I have come to understand why Jacob set up a stone and poured a drink offering upon it. At Bethel, we who are interested only in the house of God spontaneously become a drink offering.

According to Romans 16:3-5, Aquila and Priscilla were such people. This couple was absolute for the local churches. Their only interest was the church, and they were willing to be martyred for it. They risked their necks for the Apostle Paul and for the churches. Because Aquila and Priscilla risked their necks for the churches and were interested only in the churches, they were undoubtedly a drink offering; they were ready to be poured out.

We need to go over the verses regarding the drink offering again and again. I repeat that the drink offering is in addition to the basic offerings we have experienced. We should not say that it is sufficient merely to have the burnt offering, the meal offering, the peace offering, the sin offering, and the trespass offering. If this is our attitude, then we are poor in experience. Our burnt offering must be accompanied by the drink offering. The basic offering, which is Christ Himself, must always be complemented by a matching offering, the drink offering. The matching offering is not merely Christ Himself; it is the Christ who has saturated us and who has made us one with Him. We must be those who have the drink offering to match the basic offerings. The larger our offering is, the larger our matching offering must be. If we offer only the basic offerings, our offerings will be poor and short of experience. We need to offer Christ daily as our basic offerings. At the same time we must have something to match these offerings. The matching offering comes from our experience of the basic offerings. The more the basic offerings make us one with Christ, the more we become the matching offering, the drink offering. After we have come to this point, we are fully assured that we are at Bethel.

If we fit together the verses concerning the drink offering like the pieces of a jigsaw puzzle, we shall see that the drink offering is mainly for the church. The first mention of the drink offering is in Genesis 35. The first mention of a matter determines the principle of that matter in the Scriptures. The drink offering is first mentioned in relation to God's building, for this offering was poured out upon the pillar. If we read about the drink offering in Exodus, Leviticus, and Numbers without having Genesis 35:14 as a basis, we shall not realize that the drink offering is for the building of God. But we must return to the first mention of the drink offering, where we see that it was not only for the worship of God, but also for the building of Bethel. The last mention of the drink offering is 2 Timothy 4:6. Here the drink offering is also for the church, for Bethel. Therefore, from the first mention to the last, the drink offering is mainly for God's building, not mainly for the worship of God. Apparently, the drink offering is for worship; actually, it is for the house of God, for the building of the pillar, the signboard of God's temple.

We need to have a good number of saints who are ready to be poured out upon God's building. This is genuine martyrdom. Martyrdom is the pouring out of a drink offering full of the experience of Christ. When you are filled to the brim with the experience of Christ, then you will be ready to be poured out, to be martyred, for the building of God. We need this in the Lord's recovery today. We are not told whether or not Aquila and Priscilla were martyred. But we know for certain that in their spirit, attitude, and way of life they had already been martyred. Hence, they were a genuine drink offering, not only for the worship of God, but even the more for God's building.

When Jacob poured the drink offering upon the pillar, he undoubtedly felt that he was worshipping God. To him, the pouring out of that offering was an act of worship. The word "offering" denotes something related to the worship of God. This worship, however, is not a religious ritual; it is for God's building. Today in the Lord's recovery we need many saints to experience Christ to the extent that they are so filled with Him and saturated with Him as wine that they become the very wine to be poured out upon God's building for His worship and satisfaction in His building. This is the meaning of the drink offering.

(3) Pouring Oil upon the Pillar

Genesis 35:14 also tells us that Jacob poured oil upon the pillar. He did this after he had poured the drink offering upon it. I used to think that Jacob was mistaken in doing this and that he should have poured the oil first. But Jacob was not mistaken. According to our experience, it is the pouring out of the drink offering that brings in the oil. If we are ready to be poured out as a drink offering, we are also ready to experience the outpouring of the Spirit. The more we are prepared to be poured out as a drink offering, the more of the oil we shall enjoy.

After the pillar was set up, it was sanctified by being anointed with oil. The same was true of the tabernacle. After it was erected, it was sanctified by the holy anointing oil (Exo. 40:9). The pillar was set up, the drink offering was poured upon it, and then the pillar was sanctified by the oil. The oil poured upon the pillar sealed it. This simply means that the pillar was sanctified. The pouring out of the oil caused the building of God to be absolutely holy, sanctified, and separated unto God. If a good number of us will be ready to be poured out as a drink offering upon God's building, the Holy Spirit will immediately be present to sanctify the church. This is the sealing of the Spirit. No matter how much we experience the Holy Spirit, if we are not ready to be poured out as a drink offering, we do not have a layer of sanctifying oil upon the church. But if many are ready to be poured out as a drink offering, the church will be anointed with oil, and the church life, being sealed with a layer of oil, will be sanctified.

The real experience of the Spirit is in relation to the pouring out of the drink offering. Consider the experience of the one hundred and twenty on the day of Pentecost. As we all know, on the day of Pentecost the Holy Spirit was poured out (Acts 2:33). Before this took place, the one hundred and twenty were ready to be poured out as a drink offering. When Peter stood up with the eleven, he was already being poured out. The result was that the oil, the Holy Spirit, came down upon them. The oil did not come before they were ready to be poured out as a drink offering. You may remark that Peter was not martyred at that time. This, of course, is true. But you must realize that he stood there like a martyr and risked his neck. Although the Jewish religionists were opposing him, he was not afraid of them. In the eyes of the angels, all the hundred and twenty were already being poured out as a drink offering. Thus, the oil was poured out to sanctify and to seal them. On that day the church at Jerusalem was anointed with a layer of heavenly oil. Unlike today's Christian organizations, the church was holy, separated, and sanctified. May all the churches in the Lord's recovery be like this. I hope that a good number of saints will be already poured out as a drink offering so that the Holy Spirit as the heavenly oil will come upon the church to seal it, sanctify it, and make it absolutely separated to God. This is the experience at Bethel.

(4) Realizing Bethel

After Jacob did all these things at Bethel, he called the name of the place Bethel (35:15), indicating that he realized that this was the house of God where God spoke to him (28:13-15). Today, the church is the house of God (1 Tim. 3:15; Heb. 3:6). Like Jacob at Bethel, we also must have the practical experiences for the church life. We must build an altar of consecration, we must set up a pillar for God's building, and we must be ready to be poured out as a drink offering upon God's building that the divine oil may be poured upon it to sanctify it for God. To do this is to realize the practical church life.

LIFE-STUDY OF GENESIS

MESSAGE NINETY

BEING TRANSFORMED

(10)

After remaining in Bethel for quite a long time, Jacob journeyed on from there (35:16). Apparently, this journey away from Bethel was not a positive move. But Jacob's leaving Bethel does not mean that he left the house of God; it means that he was going on in his spiritual experience. Although he had come to Bethel, had stayed there, and had done certain things there, he still had to go on.

We have seen that Genesis is a book of seeds and pictures. We need to understand the significance of all these seeds and pictures. The picture of Abraham, Isaac, and Jacob is a portrait of our spiritual life. The experience of these three men is a picture of the spiritual life of one person following the Lord.

6) Deeper and More Personal Dealings

a) The Death of Rachel

As Jacob was journeying on from Bethel, he experienced a very deep and personal dealing: his beloved wife, Rachel, died as she was giving birth to Jacob's last son, Benjamin (35:16-20). This experience was a matter related to both death and birth, a matter of both loss and gain. Jacob lost Rachel and gained Benjamin. If you had to make the choice, would you prefer to keep the mother or to gain the son? The popular Christian concept is to have both the mother and the son. But in the divine economy, if you would gain the last son, you must let go of the mother. Without loss there can be no gain, and without death there can be no birth. Birth comes out of death, for apart from death there is no resurrection. If Rachel had not died, Benjamin could never have come forth.

Rachel represents Jacob's natural choice. Although Jacob had four wives, only Rachel was the natural and original choice according to the desire of Jacob's heart. He was forced to accept Leah and also constrained to take the two maids, Bilhah and Zilpah. But Leah and the two maids were not the choice of Jacob's heart. If you read Genesis carefully, you will see that Jacob's heart was absolutely set on Rachel; he had no heart for the other three. Recall what Jacob did when he feared an attack of Esau and his men. He put the two handmaids and their children at the front, followed by Leah and her children in the middle, and Rachel and Joseph at the rear (33:1-2). The fact that Jacob placed Rachel and Joseph at the rear to protect them in case of attack reveals that Jacob's heart was set on Rachel.

Everything in the Bible is purposeful. The death of Rachel is recorded here in chapter thirty-five with a definite purpose. As Jacob was taking his journey, he must have been joyful knowing that Rachel was pregnant again. Perhaps he expected his beloved wife to give him another boy. But as Rachel was giving birth to her second child, she died, and Jacob's natural choice, the desire of his heart, was taken away from him.

Before the experience at Bethel, God tolerated Jacob's natural choice, allowing him to have his heart's desire. But after the experience at Bethel, his natural choice was taken from him. Many of us can testify that before we experienced the church life, we still had our natural concept, natural choice, and natural desire. God even bestowed His blessing upon them. Consider, for example, the birth of Rachel's first child, Joseph. When Joseph was born, Jacob was very happy and might have said, "This is God's blessing upon the desire of my heart. God has blessed my choice." However, after his experience at Bethel, Jacob lost his natural choice.

After you experience the church life, your natural choice must be left behind. Before you came into the church, you still had your natural choice, and God tolerated it. But after experiencing the church life to a certain extent, God will tolerate it no longer. I hope that this will not frighten the young people and cause them to draw back from the experience at

Bethel. When they hear about this, some may say, "If this will happen, I will never come to Bethel. Rather, I will stay on the other side of Bethel and go no further. Then I will not lose my natural choice." Yes, after you have had some experience at Bethel, you will lose your natural choice, but you will gain Benjamin, who is a type of Christ.

(1) Bringing In Christ as the Son of Sorrow (Benoni) and as the Son of the Right Hand (Benjamin)

Verse 18 says, "And it came to pass, as her soul was in departing, (for she died,) that she called his name Benoni: but his father called him Benjamin." This child was given two names, one from his mother and one from his father. Benoni means "the son of sorrow." Rachel gave him this name because she was suffering and in sorrow. But Jacob immediately changed his name to Benjamin, which means "the son of the right hand." In this whole universe there is only One who is both the Son of sorrow and the Son of the right hand—and that One is Christ. On the one hand Christ is Benoni, and on the other hand He is Benjamin. Christ is a wonderful Person with these two aspects. No one has suffered as much sorrow as Christ, and no one has been exalted as high as Christ. Isaiah 53:3 describes Him as "a man of sorrows," Acts 2:33 says that He has been "exalted to the right hand of God," and Hebrews 1:3 says that He is seated "on the right hand of the Majesty on high." Firstly, Jesus was the Son of sorrow, the Son of suffering. Rachel was not the only one to experience this sorrow; Mary, the mother of Christ, also experienced it. According to Luke 2:35, her soul was pierced by the sufferings of her son. But after thirty-three and a half years, in resurrection and ascension Christ became the Son of the right hand of God. Hence, no one can deny that Benjamin was a type of the suffering and exalted Christ.

Suppose you had been Jacob. Would you have been willing to gain this Christ at the cost of losing the desire of your heart? As long as you stay in the church, experience Bethel, set up a pillar, and pour yourself out upon it as a drink offering, you will have no choice. Rachel must die that Benjamin might be born. Hallelujah, Rachel has gone and Benjamin has come!

More than fifty years ago, I heard messages and read books about expressing Christ and manifesting Him. But I was bothered by the fact that I did not know how to lift up Christ or to express Him. For many years I was not able to find the way. Some said that in order to express Christ we must be crucified. But how can a person crucify himself? It is impossible for anyone to nail himself to the cross. Eventually I learned that the way to lift up Christ and to express Him is in the church life. Through the church life "Rachel" will have a marvelous and encouraging delivery, dying that the wonderful Christ may come forth. I have tried every way to uplift and express Christ, and I can testify strongly that none of these ways has been effective. However, after I came to the church and stayed here for a period of time, my "Rachel," my natural choice, was taken away, and Benjamin was brought forth.

The record in the Bible of the death of Rachel and the birth of Benjamin is surely admirable. What a wonderful record it is! Why did Rachel's death not come before Jacob's experience at Bethel? Certainly this was according to the sovereignty of God. In God's sovereignty, Rachel's death occurred right after Jacob's marvelous experience at Bethel. In verse 16 Jacob must have been full of joy from his experiences at Bethel. Also, he eagerly anticipated the birth of another child of his beloved wife, Rachel. But as Rachel's child was being born, Jacob's natural choice was dying. Although Rachel named her second son Benoni, a name of sorrow, Jacob immediately changed the name to Benjamin, a name of encouragement. The fact that Jacob changed the name of his son proves that he was not disappointed or discouraged by the loss of Rachel. Instead of being despondent, he was filled with assurance, faith, and hope. Jacob seemed to say, "No, his name must be Benjamin. He is not the son of sorrow—he is the son of the right hand." What faith and hope Jacob had! However, if this had taken place before Jacob's experience at Bethel, he would have said, "Amen, his name must be Benoni because he is a son of sorrow. Indeed, this experience is sorrowful." But after his experience at Bethel, Jacob was a transformed person.

Verse 21 indicates that Jacob had truly been transformed: "And Israel journeyed, and spread his tent beyond the tower of Edar." Here, after the death of Rachel and the birth of Benjamin, Jacob is actually called Israel for the first time. We are not told that Jacob journeyed, but that Israel journeyed. By that time Jacob had become a transformed person. Prior to this, his name had been changed from Jacob to Israel (32:27-28; 35:10), but he had never actually been called by his new name.

(2) Rachel Having Brought Forth Joseph, a Nazarite, a Type of Christ

Jacob had twelve sons: six, including Levi with the priesthood and Judah with the kingship, were born of Leah; two, Joseph and Benjamin, were born of Rachel; two, Dan, the worst, and Naphtali, one of the best, were born of Bilhah; and two others, Gad and Asher, were born of Zilpah (vv. 22-26). Benjamin and Joseph, the two sons of Rachel, are both types of Christ. Although Joseph was born first, in typology he is the continuation of Benjamin. The record of Joseph's birth does not indicate that he is a type of Christ. But, as we have seen, the birth of Benjamin clearly reveals that he is a type of Christ. Benjamin, the son of sorrow and the son of the right hand, is continued by Joseph. From chapter thirty-seven to the end of the book of Genesis, we have the record of Joseph's life. Joseph, a Nazarite, one separated unto God, is surely a type of Christ (49:26, "separate" in Hebrew is "the Nazarite").

Joseph typified Christ as both the Son of sorrow and the Son of the right hand. After his suffering and exaltation, Joseph was seated next to Pharaoh on the throne. When we come to the record of Joseph, we shall see that in every respect he is a type of Christ. For the time being, one example is sufficient to illustrate this. When Joseph was in prison he had two companions (40:1-4). Later, one of these companions was saved and the other perished (40:20-22). When the Lord Jesus was on the cross, He was accompanied by two thieves, one of whom was saved and one of whom was lost (Luke

23:32-33, 39-43). How marvelous is this typology! During the first part of his life, Joseph suffered as the son of sorrow. During the second part of his life, he was exalted to be the son of the right hand. He was lifted up to the throne at the right hand of Pharaoh and was empowered to administer the life supply to all the people. However, as we have pointed out, in typology Joseph is the continuation of Benjamin, the son of sorrow who became the son of the right hand.

Benjamin and Joseph were born of Rachel, Jacob's natural choice. According to God's ordination, natural things are not wrong. God has ordained that we get married. Although married life is natural, it is ordained by God. Never say that natural things are not good. If you say this, then you should stop eating, for eating is a natural necessity ordained by God. Young people often say, "Why must we be troubled with food and clothing? And why do we need to sleep? If God had created us without the need for food, clothing, and sleep, life would be wonderful. Besides, who likes to stand in front of a hot oven, and who enjoys washing dishes? How good it would be if we were not bothered by such things. I wish we could exist without all these necessities." Nevertheless, God has ordained marriage, eating, sleeping, and clothing. Although these things are natural, they have been ordained by God.

Like all men, Jacob needed a wife. When he came to the home of his uncle Laban in Padan-aram, the first person he met was Rachel (29:9-11), and she immediately became his choice. Certainly this was sovereignly arranged by God. As Jacob looked at Rachel, he might have said, "This is my choice." Jacob loved Rachel and agreed to serve Laban seven years for her (29:18-20). God was sovereign in causing Jacob to meet Rachel first, and He was also sovereign in allowing Laban to play a trick on Jacob. Although Laban had betrothed Rachel to Jacob, at the time of the marriage he gave him Leah instead (29:21-25). Laban's deceitfulness frustrated Jacob from having his choice. Jacob then made a deal with Laban to serve another seven years for Rachel. In order to have his choice he was willing to suffer this. As Jacob was working those years for Rachel, every time he saw her, he must have yearned for her. But he could not have her. Although none of us would have been this patient, Jacob patiently waited out this time, and eventually Rachel was given to him.

This record is full of spiritual meaning. God has ordained us to have our natural choice. But under God's sovereignty we must be kept from having it for a period of time. On the one hand, Jacob was frustrated from having his natural choice; on the other hand, he was permitted to have it. This means that although God has ordained something for us, He will not allow us to have it according to our way and according to our time. Undoubtedly, Rachel was ordained by God for Jacob. But God did not permit Jacob to have Rachel according to his way and his time. Jacob wanted to have Rachel immediately. After Jacob finally had her, he certainly desired to keep her for the rest of his life. However, at a certain point God seemed to say, "Jacob, I shall take Rachel away from you." I do not speak this in vain. From my experience I know it is real.

God has ordained us to have our natural choice, but not according to our way and our time. You may wonder why God bothers us like this. His one purpose in doing it is to bring forth Christ. God has ordained you to have a wife, but He will not allow you to have her in your way and at your time. His purpose is not to make you suffer. God is not cruel. His purpose is to bring forth Christ. God has also ordained you to eat, but not to eat in your way. Even in this, God's purpose is to bring forth Christ.

Some of you know that I am very fond of dessert, especially ice cream. But God has sovereignly placed me under the controlling hand of my dear wife. When I do get to eat ice cream, it is not according to my way or at my time. My wife can testify that many times I long to eat ice cream at noon, but she tells me to wait until dinner. By this I have learned the lesson of not getting my natural choice in my way and at my time, but according to His way and His time. His purpose in this is not to make me suffer; it is to bring forth Christ. Whenever my dear wife tells me to wait until dinner time to eat ice cream, I simply return to my study. I never quarrel with her about it. This example from my experience illustrates the principle.

Suppose, being a man and having the strength to fight, I

would say to my wife, "This is my home, this is my family, and you are my wife. Serve me ice cream right now! I refuse to wait until dinner time!" If I lived like this, there would be no bringing forth of Christ. There would be no Benjamin and no Joseph.

Recently I encouraged the young people to gain the highest education. Many now have this ambition. I know some young lovers of the Lord who made the choice to get a good education. Although they did get the education they desired, they did not get it according to their way or according to their time, but according to God's way and God's time. Apparently, this caused them a measure of suffering. But God's purpose is not to cause suffering—it is to bring forth Christ, to bring forth Benjamin and Joseph.

We all must learn that we are not in our own hands. Rather, we are in the hands of the Lord. As long as we are His chosen ones and we love Him, we are in His hands. He will bring us to Bethel, and we shall stay at Bethel under His hand. Sooner or later, we shall journey on, and at His time His hand will take away our desire, our choice, that Benjamin may come forth.

The book of Genesis issues in Joseph on the throne with power and authority to administer the life supply to all people. This issue proceeds directly out of Jacob's experience with Rachel. Without Jacob's experience with Rachel, neither Benjamin nor Joseph could have come into being. I repeat, the consummation of the whole book of Genesis comes out of Jacob's relationship with Rachel. The proper experience of Jacob with Rachel is that our natural choice, ordained by God, is not given to us according to our way and our time, but according to God's way and God's time. Whatever our choice is—whether it is related to marriage, eating, or manner of dress—it will be given in the Lord's way and in His time.

Even as you are dressing yourself, you need to say, "Lord, what is Your way? What is Your time?" Young people, all your daily needs and necessities have been ordained by God. But do not expect to get anything according to your way and your time. That would never bring forth Christ. If you would be used by God to bring forth Christ, your necessities must be given you, not according to your way and your time, but according to God's way and God's time.

The Bible does not say that Jacob mourned after the death of Rachel. Jacob was clear that the loss of his wife was under the sovereign hand of God. Instead of being disappointed, he was greatly encouraged, immediately changing his son's name from "the son of sorrow" to "the son of the right hand." In this matter Jacob was not weak; he was very strong, knowing that Rachel's death was of God. This is confirmed by the fact that the Holy Spirit called him Israel in verse 21. This proves that he was fully transformed.

Prior to chapter thirty-five, Jacob had passed through many dealings, especially during his twenty years with Laban. But those dealings were not as deep and as personal as the loss of his dear wife. This dealing was deep and personal, and it touched the very depths of his being. After you have known the church life to a certain degree, you also will have such an experience. Something will happen that will touch you, not superficially, but deeply. Your heart's choice will be taken away so that you may bring forth Christ as Benjamin and as Joseph. Thank the Lord for this clear picture and for this word. I believe that a good number of us need this message just at this time.

b) The Defilement of Jacob's Concubine, Rachel's Maidservant, Having Changed the Birthright

The loss of Rachel was not the only painful thing that happened to Jacob as he journeyed from Bethel. Another deep hurt was the defilement of Jacob's concubine by Reuben (v. 22). This also was a heart-touching and heart-rending experience. Verse 22 contains the very significant words, "And Israel heard it." You may wonder how such an immoral deed could have taken place in this godly family. Nevertheless, it happened.

The defilement of Jacob's concubine by Reuben caused the birthright to be changed (1 Chron. 5:1; Gen. 48:22). Reuben, born of Leah, was the firstborn. Actually and practically as the firstborn son he was the one to inherit the birthright. But due to the fact that he defiled Jacob's concubine, he lost his birthright, and the birthright was given to Joseph.

After the relationship between Jacob and Rachel had been fully dealt with, one of their sons was given the birthright. This is very meaningful. Deep in Jacob's heart, he felt that Rachel, not Leah, was his wife. Therefore, according to Jacob, the firstborn should not have been Reuben, but Joseph. Although it was of God that Reuben was the firstborn, it was not according to the desire of Jacob's heart. God had sovereignly caused Jacob to marry Leah and to bring forth Reuben. However, Jacob's heart was set on Rachel and Joseph. In his eyes, Joseph was truly the firstborn. God is fair. Having forced Jacob to marry Leah and to bring forth the firstborn through her, He eventually loosed His hand and let Reuben go. Reuben fell, and the birthright was adjusted.

This should come as a comfort to you. You may be concerned about God's dealing so thoroughly with your natural choice, with the desire of your heart. But God will eventually act to adjust the situation. By the loss of Rachel Jacob gained a second son who typified Christ, and by the defilement caused by Reuben the birthright was adjusted. We should not be troubled by what happens to us. Rather, we all must believe that everything is under the sovereign hand of God. The defilement of Jacob's concubine by Reuben was shameful, but even such a shameful thing was used to bring a positive result. The birthright should not have gone to Reuben, but according to natural birth he did possess it. Thus, in His sovereignty, God allowed Reuben to fall that the birthright might be transferred to the proper person. How marvelous this is! However, never use God's sovereignty as an excuse to say, "Let us do evil that good may come."

7) *Entering into Fellowship*

After experiencing these deeper and more personal dealings, Jacob entered into full fellowship with the Lord at Hebron (v. 27). The fellowship at Hebron means intimacy, peace, satisfaction, and joy. It is wonderful to be in the church life. However, at the beginning of our experience in the church life, we do not have full fellowship. This fellowship is at Hebron. Many who are in the church life today are not in a spiritual situation that is intimate, peaceful, satisfying, and joyful. Although you are in the church life, you still need to journey on, passing through deeper and more personal dealings until you come to Hebron and enter into full fellowship with the Lord. In this fellowship you will have complete joy, satisfaction, peace, and intimacy between you and the Lord.

Verse 27 says, "And Jacob came unto Isaac his father unto Mamre, unto Kiriath-arba, which is Hebron, where Abraham and Isaac sojourned." Abraham had come to Shechem (12:6), had passed through Bethel (12:8), and had dwelt in Hebron (13:18; 18:1), and Isaac spent nearly his whole life in Hebron. Jacob, therefore, followed Abraham's footsteps to come to Shechem (33:18), to pass through Bethel (35:6), and to dwell in Hebron. We all need to come to Hebron. Although we are in the church life, we do not have rest, full peace, satisfaction, joy, and intimacy until we journey onward in our spirit to Hebron. Here in Hebron we enjoy wonderful intimacy with the Lord. Hebron is also the place where we mature in life. In 37:1, Jacob began to mature because he was in Hebron.

8) Released from the Tie with His Father

In verses 28 and 29 we are told of the death of Isaac. When Jacob was at Hebron, his last earthly tie, the tie with his father, was cut. Some may say, "We all must honor our parents. Why would you say that the tie was cut when Jacob's father died?" On the one hand, it is good to have our parents with us, but on the other hand, every relationship is a tie. After Jacob came to Hebron and entered into full rest, God took away his father and set him completely free from every earthly tie. At the end of chapter thirty-five we see a person completely transformed and set free. Jacob is now in Hebron, in full rest, joy, satisfaction, intimacy, and fellowship with the Lord. At Hebron there is nothing between Jacob and the Lord. Here he can sing, "Nothing between, Lord, nothing between." In Jacob we see a person thoroughly dealt with by God and wholly adjusted by Him. Every tie has been cut and he is fully free to enjoy intimate fellowship with the Lord in Hebron.

LIFE-STUDY OF GENESIS

MESSAGE NINETY-ONE

THE THREE PILLARS AND THE ONE TOWER IN JACOB'S LIFE

As we trace the history of Jacob, we see that in his life there were three pillars and one tower. Although Jacob set up pillars four times, he erected them in just three places—at Gilead, at Bethel, and on the way to Bethlehem (31:45; 28:18, 22; 35:14, 20). Because Jacob set up pillars in three places, twice setting up a pillar at Bethel, there were actually three pillars in his life as landmarks of his experience. In addition to these three pillars, Jacob also experienced a tower, the tower of Eder (35:21). We must believe that everything recorded in the Bible has a special significance. In this message we must consider, as a parenthesis, the significance of the three pillars and the one tower in Jacob's life.

I. THE THREE PILLARS

A. The Pillar at Gilead

The three pillars set up by Jacob were landmarks in his life. They divided his life into three sections. In the first section Jacob experienced God's care. From the day of his birth, he was under God's care. However, Jacob, a supplanter, a heel-holder, thought he was under his own care. Eventually he realized that he was not under his own care, but under God's care. If Jacob had been under his own care, he would not have been able to deal with his cunning uncle, Laban, or to confront his strong brother, Esau. Rather, he would have been totally defeated by Laban or absolutely destroyed by Esau. But because Jacob was under God's care, neither Laban nor Esau could harm him. Although Jacob did everything possible to take care of himself, he gradually learned that he was under God's care.

Recall how Jacob left Laban. He did not leave in a glorious way; rather he was afraid of Laban and stole away from him in a somewhat shameful manner (31:20-21). In doing so "Jacob stole the heart of Laban the Syrian" (31:20, Heb.). Thinking that he had to flee for his own protection, Jacob secretly stole away from Laban. Later Jacob realized that he was not protected by his skill, but by God's care. Although Laban did not know of Jacob's flight until three days later, he still pursued him until he caught up with him (31:23). The night before Laban overtook Jacob, God said to him, "Take heed that thou speak not to Jacob from good to bad" (31:24, Heb.). God seemed to be telling Laban, "Don't do anything to Jacob. You must leave him in My hands." Laban was unwise in relating to Jacob what God had told him the previous night (31:29). If Laban had not divulged this, he could have made a deal with Jacob. Jacob used what God had told Laban as the ground to rebuke him, saying, "Except the God of my father, the God of Abraham, and the fear of Isaac, had been with me, surely thou hadst sent me away now empty. God hath seen mine affliction and the labor of my hands, and rebuked thee yesternight" (31:42). As Jacob was rebuking Laban, deep in his heart he might have felt grateful to God for protecting him. God was sovereign over all his circumstances for his existence.

Laban then said to Jacob, "Now therefore come thou, let us make a covenant, I and thou; and let it be for a witness between me and thee" (31:44). Jacob responded to Laban's proposal by taking a stone and setting it up for a pillar (31:45). Although Laban intended to pile up a heap of stones, Jacob set up a pillar. This pillar was a testimony of God's care of Jacob. Jacob had come to see that his living was altogether under the care of God. Hence, he set up this pillar as a strong testimony of God's care for him.

Jacob was under God's care for more than twenty years. Although he was in Laban's squeezing hand for such a long time (Laban changed his wages ten times—31:41), God was with him all the while, and His hand was upon him. Therefore, as Jacob was making a deal with Laban, he set up a pillar to testify that he was under God's care. This pillar was for Jacob's existence. Many of us have also set up such a pillar. If you consider your own Christian experience, you will see that the first stage of your Christian life was the stage of experiencing God's care. Even before we were saved, our intention was to have God's care. When we heard the good news of the gospel, our intention in believing in the Lord Jesus was to have His care. For many years we, like Jacob, have been under the care of our heavenly Father. At the end of the first stage of our Christian life, we need to set up a pillar testifying of God's care. However, if you have been with the Lord for quite a long time, it may be too late for you to set up this pillar. Rather, you need to set up the second pillar, the pillar at Bethel.

B. The Pillar at Bethel

Years before Jacob set up this pillar at Gilead, he had set up a pillar at Bethel (28:18, 22). However, Jacob set up that pillar immediately after having a dream. Once again we see that Jacob's biography is also our biography. Not long after we were saved, we heard something about the house of God and we responded to what we heard. But everything we heard and did was like a dream. We did not actually experience the house of God. In Genesis 28 Jacob had a dream. After that dream, he had a real experience, not of the house of God, but of the care of God. At the end of this stage of his experience he set up a pillar at Gilead as a landmark to testify of God's care. As we shall see, in our Christian life we need three pillars, three landmarks, the first of which is the pillar testifying of God's care for us.

After Jacob had left Padan-aram and had returned to the good land, he did not go directly to Bethel. God had to intervene and call him to Bethel, saying, "Arise, go up to Bethel, and dwell there: and make there an altar unto God, that appeared unto thee when thou fleddest from the face of Esau thy brother" (35:1). This indicates that Jacob had no intention of fulfilling the vow he had made to God at Bethel twenty years earlier. He had probably forgotten it. Instead of journeying directly to Bethel to fulfill his vow, Jacob journeyed to Succoth, where he built a house for himself and made booths for his cattle (33:17). Later he traveled to Shechem, where he bought a parcel of land and spread his tent (33:18-19). After the serious trouble following the defilement of Jacob's daughter, Dinah, God came in and told Jacob to arise and to go up to Bethel. When Jacob came to Bethel the second time, he did not have a dream. He had been ordered by God to go there, to dwell there, and to build an altar there to the God who had appeared to him when he was fleeing from Esau. At Bethel Jacob consecrated himself to God so that He might fulfill His purpose of having Bethel, the house of God. Here at Bethel Jacob set up the second pillar, the second landmark in his life (35:14). As 28:22 indicates, the pillar in Bethel was called the house of God. Therefore, the first pillar was a testimony of God's care, and the second was a testimony of God's house.

Because Jacob's history is also our experience, we all must worship the Lord. Many of us have set up pillars both at Gilead and at Bethel. We can testify, not only of God's care, but also of God's house. Jacob's first pillar was a testimony of God's care for his existence. When Jacob, a poor supplanter, arrived at Laban's house, he had nothing. But when he returned to the good land, he had acquired great riches. He had armies of people and armies of flocks and herds. In his vow made in 28:20 and 21, Jacob said, "If God will be with me, and will keep me in this way that I go, and will give me bread to eat, and raiment to put on, so that I come again to my father's house in peace; then shall the Lord be my God." In other words, Jacob was actually saying, "If the Lord will not give me food and clothing, and if He will not bring me back to my father's house in peace, then I will not take Him as my God. Rather, I will forget about Him." What a deal Jacob had made with God! Nevertheless, God met all the conditions of Jacob's vow, supplying him with food and clothing, giving him peace, and even increasing him with armies of people and flocks. But here in chapter thirty-five God seemed to be saying, "Jacob, now you must go to Bethel. You should no longer be concerned for your food, your clothing, and your peace. You must take care of Me and My house. Jacob, I have been taking care of you for years. Beginning now, you must take care of Me."

Many of us can testify that years ago we set up a pillar at Gilead. At that time our testimony concerned God's care for us. We testified that our God was faithful, kind, gracious, and rich. But today our testimony is not that of the first pillar, the testimony of God's care; it is the second pillar, the testimony of God's house. However, not many Christians today take care of God's house. Most are primarily concerned about their own needs, and the pillar they set up is only a testimony of God's care. Very few experientially set up a pillar to testify of God's house. To have the pillar of God's care without the pillar of God's house is not normal. As today's Jacobs, we must set up the second pillar for God's building. Praise the Lord that many of us have done so. In our Christian life we have not only the first section, the section of God's care, but also the second section, the section of God's house. Nevertheless, we must journey on and set up the third pillar.

C. The Pillar on the Way to Bethlehem

My burden in this message is the third pillar, the pillar on the way to Bethlehem (35:16-20). At Bethel Jacob built an altar and set up a pillar. Not only did he answer God's call; he also consecrated himself to God for the fulfillment of His desire to have Bethel. However, Jacob's life did not end at 35:15. Verse 16 says that he journeyed on from Bethel. As Jacob was journeying on, he had an experience that was a matter of both joy and suffering, a matter of both gain and loss. Jacob gained a son, Benjamin, and he lost his beloved wife, Rachel. If you had to make the choice, would you prefer to gain the son or to keep the wife? In order to gain the son, you must sacrifice your wife, and in order to keep your wife, you must be denied the son. Although Jacob had eleven sons, not one of them was a full type of Christ. He had had many experiences, but not one of them was adequate to bring forth Christ. Thus, he was confronted with a choice—to keep Rachel or to gain Benjamin. This is a crucial matter, and we all must face it.

Actually, the choice was not made by Jacob. If he had preferred to keep Rachel, he could not have done so. Furthermore, if he had wanted to reject Benjamin, he would not have been able to do this. Both the death of Rachel and the birth of Benjamin were in the hand of God.

Leah, the one Jacob did not love so much, had brought forth six sons. Rachel, the object of Jacob's love, had brought forth only one son—Joseph, whose name means "addition." When Joseph was born, Rachel expected to have a second son and said, "The Lord shall add to me another son" (30:24). In her expectation of having another son, she seemed to be saying, "God has taken away my reproach and has given me a son. But one son is not sufficient. I want another one. Hence, I shall call the name of my first son Joseph." This should imply a prayer, a prayer answered at the cost of Rachel's life. Rachel had such a prayer in 30:24, and the answer came in 35:18. In order to gain her desire, Rachel had to lose her own life. In 30:24 she did not actually realize what she was saying. Rachel expected that God would give her a second son, but she did not know that this would cost her her life. Many of us have done the same thing. We prayed for a particular matter without knowing what it would cost to have our prayer answered.

At the time of the delivery of Rachel's second child, Jacob must have been happy. But he suddenly realized that Rachel, the desire of his heart, was dying. Benjamin was coming, but Rachel was departing. The fact that the birth of Benjamin and the death of Rachel occurred simultaneously means that Jacob gained a son by losing his natural choice. The crucial point in this message is that Jacob gained Christ through the loss of his natural choice. The third pillar in Jacob's life was a testimony of God's dealing with his natural choice.

It is wonderful to have the testimony of God's care and the testimony of the house of God. But not even the house of God is God's ultimate goal. God's ultimate goal is to express Christ. The expression of Christ is not an individual matter; it is a corporate matter in the house of God. The church as the house of God is for the expression of Christ. In order to express Christ, we must have the church. However, most Christians think they can express Christ without the church. But it is impossible to express Christ adequately apart from the church. In addition to the pillar of God's care and the pillar of God's house, we must have the third pillar, the pillar for the corporate expression of Christ. This pillar is costly.

Genesis 35:20 says that Jacob set a pillar upon Rachel's grave, and that this "is the pillar of Rachel's grave unto this day." This grave marked the death of Jacob's natural choice, the choice of his heart. Rachel was the first person Jacob met when he arrived at Laban's home, and he immediately fell in love with her. He did everything necessary to have her as his wife, and eventually she was given to him. Rachel did not die of old age; she died prematurely in childbirth. The fact that she was still able to bear children indicates that she was not in her old age. All of Leah's six deliveries of her sons and the one of her daughter went very well, but Rachel died in giving birth to her second child. Her death was allowed by God.

The death of Rachel signifies the death of our natural choice. The first two pillars we set up are not for us to have a happy life—they are for us to exist to build the house of God for the expression of Christ. Although Jacob had eleven sons, not one of them was a complete type of Christ. Not one of them was the son of sorrow and the son of the right hand. Joseph was excellent, but prior to the birth of Benjamin, he was not a type of Christ. In typology Joseph is the continuation of Benjamin. This implies that no matter how many spiritual experiences we have had, up to this point, not one of them is the expression of Christ. We still need Benjamin. In order for Benjamin to be born, our natural choice, our "Rachel," must die.

God used Rachel to bring forth Benjamin. But by His using her to bring forth Benjamin, He took her away. God will also use the "Rachel" we love. But through His using our "Rachel," He takes her away from us. If you examine your experience, you will realize that God uses your choice, your desire. But by using it, He takes it from you.

Rachel's death was not only a suffering to Jacob; it was also a suffering to Rachel. Matthew 2:18 says, "A voice was heard in Ramah, weeping and great mourning, Rachel weeping for her children; and she would not be comforted, because they were no more." For many years I could not understand how Rachel, who had been buried for more than seventeen hundred years, could still be weeping. Nevertheless, this verse says that, even at the time of the birth of Christ, Rachel was still weeping over her children, all of whom were descendants of Benjamin. Benjamin truly was "the son of sorrow," and Rachel was right in giving him this name. Benjamin's birth not only took Rachel's life, but also the life of his descendants more than seventeen hundred years later. Because Christ had been born in Bethlehem, Herod slew all the children in and around Bethlehem who were two years old and younger (Matt. 2:16). Rachel was weeping over all her children, those who had been killed by Herod because of the coming of Christ. This means that Rachel suffered martyrdom for the coming of Christ. Rachel's weeping could be heard at Rama. Rachel was buried on the way to Bethlehem, and Rama is just two hundred yards from Bethlehem. Thus, Rachel's grave was close to both Bethlehem and Rama. This region was populated with the descendants of Benjamin, the son of Rachel.

After Rachel died and was buried, she still had to wait for more than seventeen hundred years to pass by. Not even losing her life for the birth of Benjamin was sufficient; she had to weep more than seventeen hundred years later for her descendants who were to suffer martyrdom for Christ. Rachel not only suffered at the time of her delivery; she even suffered more than seventeen hundred years later. The purpose of her suffering was the bringing forth of Christ. Firstly Benjamin, the type of Christ, came, and secondly Christ, the real One, came. Unlike us, God is not bound by the matter of time. For this reason, we need not be concerned about the interval of more than seventeen hundred years between the death of Rachel and the birth of Christ.

Jacob had set up a pillar at Gilead and a pillar at Bethel, but now he had to set up the third pillar on the way to Bethlehem. In our Christian life we also must have the landmark of the third pillar at Rachel's grave, the place where our natural choice is buried. Our love, our desire, and our choice will one day be brought to an end and buried. Upon the grave of our natural choice we must set up a pillar. This pillar is a signboard of the death and burial of our natural choice, the desire of our heart. Some person, some thing, or some matter we love dearly will die and be buried, and a pillar will be set up upon the grave to testify that our choice has been buried. Then we shall journey on to Bethlehem, the place where Christ is born. The pillar on the way to Bethlehem directs people to Christ.

When Jacob first met Rachel and fell in love with her, he did not know what trouble she would cause him. It was because Jacob loved Rachel that he was given Leah and the two maids, Zilpah and Bilhah. Without Leah and these two maids, he would not have had their ten sons to cause him problems. The more Jacob loved Rachel, the more trouble he had. Although Leah had given Jacob four sons, Rachel was childless and she complained to Jacob (30:1). To this Jacob said, "Am I in God's stead, who hath withheld from thee the fruit of the womb?" (30:2). Jacob seemed to be saying, "Rachel, why do you complain to me? Why don't you complain to God?" Eventually God hearkened to Rachel and gave her a son, Joseph (30:22-24). At the birth of Joseph, Rachel expected that the Lord would add to her another son. She did give birth to a second son, but as we have seen she lost her life in this childbirth. Thus, she called her second son "the son of sorrow." Furthermore, Rachel even suffered the martyrdom of the descendants of Benjamin for the coming of Christ. If you had been Jacob and could have foreseen all the troubles that would have come upon you for loving Rachel, would you still have loved her? You probably would have said, "Rachel, no matter how lovely you are, I dare not get involved with you. If I do, I will have too many troubles." Jacob of course did not know what was ahead of him. When Rachel died, he had no choice except to bury her and to set up the third pillar. He had set up the first pillar at Gilead and the second at Bethel; now he had to set up the third pillar upon Rachel's grave.

Today you may be very happy in the church life. But one day your "Rachel," the choice of your heart, will die that Benjamin might be brought forth. I am fully assured that Benjamin will be brought forth in the church life. Moreover, we must expect that even long after the death of our "Rachel," we shall still be weeping for her martyred descendants, those who suffered martyrdom for the coming of Christ.

Rachel wept because she was natural. Instead of weeping,

she should have rejoiced. If she had exercised her spirit, she would not have wept; she would have rejoiced and exulted, saying, "The one whom I have called 'the son of sorrow' is a shadow, a type, of the real Son of sorrow who will be born in Bethlehem." In the picture in Genesis 35 Rachel signifies our natural choice. To our natural choice, the birth of Benjamin is a sorrow. But to Israel it is a cause of rejoicing. The coming of Benjamin was a sorrow to Rachel, and the coming of Christ was a weeping to her. But both the coming of Benjamin and the coming of Christ were a joy to Israel. Certain things will happen in the church life that our natural man will consider a suffering and a sorrow. But to Israel, the spiritual man, these things will not be a sorrow, but a joy. Instead of weeping, there will be rejoicing.

In the first stage of our Christian life we experience God's care; in the second we experience God's house; and in the third we experience the bringing forth of Christ, the expression of Christ. The bringing forth of Christ and the expression of Christ cost us our natural life, our natural love, and our natural choice. Everything natural will eventually die and be buried. However, our natural choice will continue to suffer for a long time.

We all need three pillars, three types of testimonies. Years ago in Taipei in fellowship with the elders I pointed out that most of the testimonies in the church meetings were merely about God's care. Rarely did we hear a testimony regarding the house of God or the expression of God. At that time I did not see the picture of these three pillars as clearly as I do now. Our Christian life must have three sections: the section of God's care, the section of God's house, and the section of the expression of Christ. In the church meetings the younger ones, those who are newly saved, should testify of God's care. This is a wonderful testimony to hear from babes. But we also need some testimonies regarding God's house and the expression of Christ. If we have these three kinds of testimonies, it will be an indication that in the church we have the pillar of God's care, the pillar of God's house, and the pillar of the expression of Christ.

God's ultimate goal is the expression of Christ. This will

cost our natural choice, our natural desire, and our natural life. In neither the first nor the second pillar do we see death and the grave. Only with the third pillar do we have the death of Rachel and the grave. But the pillar erected upon Rachel's grave is on the way to Bethlehem. Thus, this pillar is on the way to Christ, and it directs people to Christ. If you would journey onward to Bethlehem, you must be on the way where there is such a pillar. Not even after you arrive in Bethlehem will there be very much joy. Instead of joy, there will be killing. Firstly, just one person, Rachel, died. Even more than seventeen hundred years later, many of her descendants were martyred that Christ might be brought forth.

I believe that in the Lord's recovery this word will be fulfilled and that we shall experience these things. May the Spirit of the Lord interpret this picture to you in a strong, clear way. What I am speaking here is no mere doctrine or interpretation. It must be the record of our life history. Many of us can say that we have the first two pillars. Perhaps soon some will have the third pillar with the death of Rachel and the grave. Along with this death and burial, there will be the coming of Christ. No matter how much martyrdom and weeping there will be, there will also be a wonderful birth—the birth of Benjamin and the birth of Christ. There will be the coming of Christ and the expression of Christ. This is God's goal and God's testimony.

II. THE ONE TOWER

After Jacob set up the third pillar, he "journeyed, and spread his tent beyond the tower of Eder" (35:21). In Hebrew Eder means "flock." In Micah 4:8 the same Hebrew phrase is rendered "tower of the flock." Here at the tower of Eder something defiling, shameful, and immoral happened to Jacob: his son Reuben committed adultery with Jacob's concubine. This did not take place at the pillar, but at the tower.

I believe that the tower of Eder, the tower of flocks, indicates the ease of life. Jacob had many flocks. As he passed by the tower of Eder, he might have considered it a good place to rest. Instead of proceeding to Hebron, his destination, he stayed by the tower of Eder. This indicates that Jacob had come to a place where he could enjoy an easy life. As he was enjoying this easy life, something sinful occurred. Sin, especially the sin of adultery, always comes in when we are at ease. The fact that Reuben committed adultery with Jacob's concubine at that place was an indication that Jacob should not have stayed there. He should have journeyed on directly to Hebron. If he had not spread his tent by the tower of Eder, probably this evil thing would not have occurred.

Although Jacob set up three pillars, there was no need for him to build the tower of Eder because it was already standing there as a snare. As you are on your way following the Lord, there will always be a tower nearby to snare you. The way to escape this trap is not to stop or even look at it. Instead of spreading your tent by the tower of Eder, you must pass it by. No matter what stage of the Christian life we are in, there is always a tower to snare us. The ease of life is always a temptation to the followers of the Lord Jesus. Every follower of the Lord realizes that his final destination is a long way off. Because the journey is so long, you expect to find a place of rest along the way. But whenever you come to a tower of flocks, you should not think of it as a place of rest—it is a snare. Pass it by and go on. No matter how exhausted you are in following the Lord, you must say, "Lord, help me. I don't want to rest at any tower. Whenever I come to a tower, I will flee from it. I will never take it as a place of rest." If you do this, you will be protected and saved from the snare.

The desire of Jacob's heart was to take Rachel as his wife. If God had not intervened through Laban, Jacob would immediately have taken Rachel as his wife. Then whoever Rachel brought forth would have been Jacob's firstborn. However, God came in and, in a sense, forced Jacob to take Leah as his wife. Thus, Reuben was actually the firstborn son, and the birthright went to him. This, however, was contrary to the desire of Jacob's heart. Furthermore, it did not seem fair. While Jacob was enjoying the ease of life at the tower of Eder, Reuben committed adultery with his father's concubine. This evil deed caused him to lose the birthright (49:3-4). First Chronicles 5:1 and 2 clearly indicate that the birthright was given to Joseph. Here we see God's sovereign adjustment of the birthright. Reuben lost the birthright because of his defilement, and Joseph gained it because of his purity (39:7-12). When Potiphar's wife tempted Joseph to commit adultery with her, he refused. Because Joseph kept himself pure, he gained the birthright Reuben had lost due to his defilement at the tower of Eder. Therefore, even Jacob's mistake was used by God to adjust the birthright. Praise the Lord for the mistake that brought about the adjustment of the birthright! But never use this fact as an excuse to say, "Let us do evil that good may come." Rather, we must bow down and worship God for His sovereignty.

The sovereign God, being fair and just, did not give all three parts of the birthright to Joseph. He gave Joseph the enjoyment of the double portion of the land, but He gave the priesthood to Leah's third son, Levi, and the kingship to her fourth son, Judah (49:10; 1 Chron. 5:2; Deut. 33:8-10). Levi received the priesthood because of his faithfulness to God (Deut. 33:9), and Judah obtained the kingship because of his love toward his brothers and his care toward his father (37:26; 43:8-9; 44:14-34). In this we see the sovereignty of God. He is behind everything and everyone. When we see this picture and how everything in it fits together, we must worship God. Hallelujah, we are under God's hand!

Jacob's biography is our history. In Jacob's life there were three pillars and one tower. We also shall have the three pillars and the one tower. I can testify that I have experienced all these things. I believe that as the years go by many of us will remember this message. Thank the Lord for the three pillars and for the one tower.

About the Author

Witness Lee was born in 1905 in northern China and raised in a Christian family. At age 19 he was fully captured for Christ and immediately consecrated himself to preach the gospel for the rest of his life. Early in his service, he met Watchman Nee, a renowned preacher, teacher, and writer. Witness Lee labored together with Watchman Nee under his direction. In 1934 Watchman Nee entrusted Witness Lee with the responsibility for his publication operation, called the Shanghai Gospel Bookroom.

Prior to the Communist takeover in 1949, Witness Lee was sent by Watchman Nee and his other co-workers to Taiwan to ensure that the things delivered to them by the Lord would not be lost. Watchman Nee instructed Witness Lee to continue the former's publishing operation abroad as the Taiwan Gospel Bookroom, which has been publicly recognized as the publisher of Watchman Nee's works outside China. Witness Lee's work in Taiwan manifested the Lord's abundant blessing. From a mere 350 believers, newly fled from the mainland, the churches in Taiwan grew to 20,000 in five years.

In 1962 Witness Lee felt led of the Lord to come to the United States, settling in California. During his 35 years of service in the U.S., he ministered in weekly meetings and weekend conferences, delivering several thousand spoken messages. Much of his speaking has since been published as over 400 titles. Many of these have been translated into over fourteen languages. He gave his last public conference in February 1997 at the age of 91.

He leaves behind a prolific presentation of the truth in the Bible. His major work, *Life-study of the Bible*, comprises over 25,000 pages of commentary on every book of the Bible from the perspective of the believers' enjoyment and experience of God's divine life in Christ through the Holy Spirit. Witness Lee was the chief editor of a new translation of the New Testament into Chinese called the Recovery Version and directed the translation of the same into English. The Recovery Version also appears in a number of other languages. He provided an extensive body of footnotes, outlines, and spiritual cross references. A radio broadcast of his messages can be heard on Christian radio stations in the United States. In 1965 Witness Lee founded Living Stream Ministry, a non-profit corporation, located in Anaheim, California, which officially presents his and Watchman Nee's ministry.

Witness Lee's ministry emphasizes the experience of Christ as life and the practical oneness of the believers as the Body of Christ. Stressing the importance of attending to both these matters, he led the churches under his care to grow in Christian life and function. He was unbending in his conviction that God's goal is not narrow sectarianism but the Body of Christ. In time, believers began to meet simply as the church in their localities in response to this conviction. In recent years a number of new churches have been raised up in Russia and in many eastern European countries.

OTHER BOOKS PUBLISHED BY
Living Stream Ministry

Titles by Witness Lee:

Abraham—Called by God	978-0-7363-0359-0
The Experience of Life	978-0-87083-417-2
The Knowledge of Life	978-0-87083-419-6
The Tree of Life	978-0-87083-300-7
The Economy of God	978-0-87083-415-8
The Divine Economy	978-0-87083-268-0
God's New Testament Economy	978-0-87083-199-7
The World Situation and God's Move	978-0-87083-092-1
Christ vs. Religion	978-0-87083-010-5
The All-inclusive Christ	978-0-87083-020-4
Gospel Outlines	978-0-87083-039-6
Character	978-0-87083-322-9
The Secret of Experiencing Christ	978-0-87083-227-7
The Life and Way for the Practice of the Church Life	978-0-87083-785-2
The Basic Revelation in the Holy Scriptures	978-0-87083-105-8
The Crucial Revelation of Life in the Scriptures	978-0-87083-372-4
The Spirit with Our Spirit	978-0-87083-798-2
Christ as the Reality	978-0-87083-047-1
The Central Line of the Divine Revelation	978-0-87083-960-3
The Full Knowledge of the Word of God	978-0-87083-289-5
Watchman Nee—A Seer of the Divine Revelation ...	978-0-87083-625-1

Titles by Watchman Nee:

How to Study the Bible	978-0-7363-0407-8
God's Overcomers	978-0-7363-0433-7
The New Covenant	978-0-7363-0088-9
The Spiritual Man • 3 volumes	978-0-7363-0269-2
Authority and Submission	978-0-7363-0185-5
The Overcoming Life	978-1-57593-817-2
The Glorious Church	978-0-87083-745-6
The Prayer Ministry of the Church	978-0-87083-860-6
The Breaking of the Outer Man and the Release ...	978-1-57593-955-1
The Mystery of Christ	978-1-57593-954-4
The God of Abraham, Isaac, and Jacob	978-0-87083-932-0
The Song of Songs	978-0-87083-872-9
The Gospel of God • 2 volumes	978-1-57593-953-7
The Normal Christian Church Life	978-0-87083-027-3
The Character of the Lord's Worker	978-1-57593-322-1
The Normal Christian Faith	978-0-87083-748-7
Watchman Nee's Testimony	978-0-87083-051-8

Available at
Christian bookstores, or contact Living Stream Ministry
2431 W. La Palma Ave. • Anaheim, CA 92801
1-800-549-5164 • www.livingstream.com

10-141-001
ISBN 978-0-87083-914-6